A Brewers Guide to Opening and Operating a Brewpub

By   Dan Woodske

A Note from the Brewpub Owner (and writer of this fine book)

Hi, I'm Dan Woodske and I own and operate Beaver Brewing Company in lovely Beaver Falls, Pennsylvania, with my equally beautiful wife Kimberly and my best friend Bemus, who is a striped 8 year-old male cat.

The Beaver Brewing Company is a brewpub and I sell 99% of the beer onsite. Almost all of that is consumed in drafts. Before I opened the pub, I ran my brewery and distributed kegs to local bars to drum up interest and get a feel for the market BEFORE I opened the pub.

I did that for about 3 years and worked on securing the location and permits for the pub in the down time. Right now, I own (at least I think) the coolest place to grab a beer in the area. It's a down-to- earth bar where all the beer served is made onsite.

I never worked in the beer business; as a matter of fact, I never worked in the food business, either. I have worked as a janitor, a maid, a newspaper ad salesman, a PR man in politics, a community developer, and a construction sales manager...not exactly a recipe for head brewer/brewpub owner.

I also didn't go to school to be a chemist. I have a degree in marketing from the University of Pittsburgh, with an area of study in Organizational Behavior (which proved to be pretty valuable, but more on that later).

Why is this information important? Because you may be cracking open this book in a similar situation...no experience in the field, no training for it, but a passionate desire to do it.

There is one caveat to all the information in this book...You *can* reach the same goal in a different way. I've been reminded several times in my life that I am NOT the world's smartest human being. This is a *guide*; if you have a better idea, PLEASE do it.

Take the information, digest it, and try to improve upon it. If you don't try to do it bigger, better, and faster than I lay it out for you, someone else will.

I have also written four other books about beer: *A Brewers Guide to Opening a Nanobrewery; Kvass: History, Health Benefits, and Recipes; Nanobrewery USA;* and *The Hop Variety Handbook: Learn more about hops, Craft Better Beer.*

Most importantly, please enjoy the journey! This is the type of business you should really ENJOY, not lose sleep over (at least not every night). If you aren't passionate about people and beer, put the book down; this isn't for you.

How to use this book

Really? How do I use a book? Before you return this from wherever you bought it, please read at least the rest of the page.

A pastor of mine told me this story years ago and I guess it stuck with me because I am going to rehash it here.

He was away on a church Youth Group camping trip. All the kids and the adults were sitting around the fire and the most elder pastor got up, threw his Bible on the ground and said, "This thing is worthless." Safe to say this caught everyone's attention.

He went on to mention a few parables of the Bible saying they, too, were worthless. He then said that every story in the Bible was just that, "a story," unless you used it.

He was proving a point. Whatever story you read or life lesson you are told is worthless...unless you apply that knowledge.

If you just read it and don't apply any of your life experiences to it, then you will find there isn't too much value to be found here.

While the Bible carries *a bit more weight* than this fine piece of work, the "story" is interchangeable. There are stories or parables from my experiences, and some charts and numbers that you can digest throughout the book. If you don't use what you have learned from this book along with *your* experience and expertise, you will find the information worthless.

So please, use this *tool* and apply what you know, what you want, and what you think your local market wants in order to build the best brewpub in your area.

One last thing... there's Homework. Yes, I am putting you to work. Throughout the book I am giving you assignments. PLEASE DO THESE! I also recommend that you do them immediately when you read them, that way you can't skip out on doing them.

What is a Brewpub?

Your state probably has its own definition (and I would investigate that right now), but here is what the Brewers Association® (BA) says about what constitutes a brewpub:

"A restaurant-brewery that sells 25% or more of its beer on site. The beer is brewed primarily for sale in the restaurant and bar. The beer is often dispensed directly from the brewery's storage tanks. Where allowed by law, brewpubs often sell beer "to go" and /or distribute to offsite accounts. Note: BA re-categorizes a company as a microbrewery if its off-site (distributed) beer sales exceed 75%."

If this isn't good enough for you, here is a really legal definition from the state of Pennsylvania where I am located. Again, please search for your state's regulations...This is directly from Title 40, aka, PA Liquor Code:

§ 3.92. Brewery pubs

 (a) The Board will be authorized to issue a brewery pub license to the holder of a brewery license. A brewery pub license may only be issued in those municipalities in which the Board may issue or transfer a malt and brewed beverage retail dispenser license.

 (b) The holder of a brewery pub license shall have all the rights and be subject to the same conditions and qualifications as those imposed on holders of a malt and brewed beverage retail dispenser license except as set forth in this section.

 (c) The brewery pub license will be issued to premises immediately adjacent to but separate and distinct from the brewery premises.

 (d) Sales of alcoholic beverages at the brewery pub premises shall be limited to sales of malt or brewed beverages produced at and owned by the brewery adjacent to it or a brewery which is under common control with the brewery pub. A brewery pub licensee may sell, for on-premises consumption, wine manufactured by the holder of a Pennsylvania limited winery license.

(e) A brewery pub license may not be issued to a brewery that has already acquired a restaurant, hotel or malt and brewed beverage retail dispenser license. If a brewery, which has a brewery pub license, applies for and acquires a restaurant, hotel or malt and brewed beverage retail dispenser license, the brewery pub license will be cancelled upon approval of the restaurant, hotel or malt and brewed beverage retail dispenser license.

(f) Any citations which may be issued under section 471 of the Liquor Code (47 P. S. § 4-471) for activity relating to the brewery pub will be issued against the brewery license.

I include this in the book because each state has WILDLY different views on what makes a brewpub. There are some states that say you have to sell food, some you can't, some you have to sell so much food...in short...do your homework. Read your state's regulations, but don't fret if you don't understand one item.

If there is something that confuses you, print out the application, circle those items that confuse you, then call the state's liquor control board and ask them your questions. They are there to help.

To sum this up, here is the Dan Woodske definition of a brewpub, *"A place where your beer is made and that beer is served in the same building. There may or may not be food there. If there isn't food, a more proper definition would be a taproom."*

- **Homework #1 – What is <u>your</u> definition of a Brewpub? How does <u>your</u> <u>state</u> define it?**

So you want to run a brewpub?

Inevitably, you have told someone other than yourself you'd like to open a brewpub. That comment was met with one of two responses: "Awesome" or "Ohhhhh...a brewpub...good luck with that, really. I wish you well."

Since it is such a unique type of business, people will either think you're awesome or a complete moron. You need to be somewhere in the middle just to keep your sanity.

Anyway, there are tons of items you have probably already thought of: What type of beers to have, the theme, tap handles, food served, your staff, tables, bar size, beer system, etc.

You're getting way ahead of yourself...or at least way ahead of me. We'll get to that, but let's kinda go in some type of order here. You can get pretty far down the road and if you haven't done one or two of the items you really NEEDED to do, you may have to start all over again.

With that said, keep thinking about all that other stuff, but be ready to adapt when it HAS to change. I'm sure you know that sometimes, well actually MOST of the time, *"Shit Happens"*. You will have to make changes at some point.

I beg of you, please at least THINK of doing what is in this book in the order in which it is laid out. It will save you plenty of time and headaches in the future.

I wrote it in a way that if you woke up this morning and decided to run a brewpub, this will walk you through the process in an order that will be beneficial to you.

Pretty much what I am trying to tell you is that there are A LOT OF MOVING PARTS HERE. You will need to plan and coordinate many of these parts *simultaneously.*

In short, don't be making tap handles when you don't even have space. You need to have your focus on the task at hand.

Again, I have actually done this myself. I didn't go to brewery school, work in a brewery, or hire a consultant and/or lawyer for $10,000 to help me navigate through this. I was (and hopefully still am) a normal person who started a brewery and grew that brewery into a brewpub.

If you take the information you are about to read in this book and actually implement it, you will be 10 steps...maybe even 11 steps ahead of everyone else.

MOST people who want to get into this business (and this may be you) get the idea in their heads and brew beer for 30 days in a row testing recipes. While that will help you make better beer, it gets you no closer to opening your place.

This brings me to the actual meat of the book...

What type of Brewpub do you want to own and why?

Before we move on, I want you to do a little exercise...not 50 push-ups, but a mental exercise.

Write down in this book why you want to run a brewpub:

If you didn't get a pen to perform this little exercise, please go back and complete this; I won't ask you to move again for the rest of the book.

Okay, I know you didn't get the pen...so really...get up and get the pen and do this...I'll wait.

Okay, you're back! Some things you may have written down: So I can quit my day job; so I can retire; to give my family a place to work for the rest of their lives; to have a good time with friends; to make money; to spend money on a business so the government doesn't take it; because I love beer.

Those are all *actual answers* I have heard from people coming in for consulting sessions. None of these are "wrong" or "bad" reasons to start a pub. They're just different.

This book should *guide* you in making all of your future decisions regarding your brewery.

Before you make any choices...

Realistically...how much money do you have (or can acquire) to invest in this? $10,000? $100,000? $1,000,000? You can establish a brewpub for all of the above numbers, but the final brewpub will look and run much differently.

Get a ballpark number in your head. This will help guide you along.

Ok, Decision Time...

You're going to have to start making some choices RIGHT NOW! You don't have to stick to them because as we already said, *"Shit Happens,"* and you may have to change your plans. But you really need to narrow down what you want to do. For the next few pages we are going to start drawing some paths for you to take.

We are still in the planning phase, so details will be a little sparse here. We'll get into numbers and all that other fun stuff later. Right now you just need to make choices on what you want your pub to look and feel like.

Please, feel free to write down your thoughts directly in the book during this phase. Some of these choices are yes/no or A/B, but they will dictate what size your space needs to be, your brewing system size, staff size, etc.

I really want you to make a choice though; don't just read and digest the info. Make a choice now; you can always change it.

Choice #1 – Food or No Food?

For some people in some states, serving food isn't an option. Many states REQUIRE brewpubs/breweries that serve onsite to serve food. That's the case for me here in Pennsylvania.

You may find that in your state you can have a taproom that doesn't have to serve food. That may be what you are looking for.

Serving food brings a WHOLE new dimension to your business. You'll probably need a wait staff, host, cooking equipment, more space, a kitchen build-out which could require code changes, a cook, a chef, plates, menus, silverware...you get the point.

Now for some of you reading this, you are all excited...a restaurant! I'll have beer cheese soup on the menu!

For others you are groaning; food is the last thing you want to be involved with.

Wherever you fall, read your state's regulations regarding brewpubs and taprooms. Some states require you to have a certain percentage of food sales to beer sales. You will need to know what your state's laws are before you do much more planning because it will greatly affect your choices down the road.

Pros of Food: Brings in more people; could give you a lunch crowd; makes people sit around in your place longer.

Cons of Food: You need more staff, equipment, money, and space; heavy turnover on food staff employees should be expected.

Choice #2 – Just your beer...or other breweries' beers?

Again, your state may dictate your option here. There are many successful brewpubs out there that serve beers from many other brewers on tap.

Some brewpubs brew on a 15-Gallon Sabco® BrewMagic™ system and have 10 other beers on tap to complement their own.

Others have 15 BBL brewhouses and serve only their beer on tap.

Some brewers out there are nanobrewers who want to run a bar and a restaurant but also have their beer available.

If you are a craft beer lover and just want to get some of your own stuff out there along with all the other great beer, you may want to serve both.

Selling your own beer will always be more profitable, but you may get more people in the door if you can have 10-12 solid craft beers on tap that people are already enjoying and are comfortable with.

This decision will also go a long way to show you what type(s) of licenses you will need. Whatever path you decide here, check with your state to see what the regulations are. (Are you starting to recognize a theme here?)

Pros: You'll never run out of beer; you'll have brands people are familiar with; easy to serve.

Cons: Your brand may get lost next to established brands, which may cut into your beer sales; people may think you are not a "true" brewpub with other beers there.

Choice #3 – Spirits and/or Wine?

Do you want a full bar? Do you want to look like Tom Cruise in *Cocktail,* swinging bottles over your head and pouring exotic drinks with umbrellas in them? Then you'll probably want to go the full bar route.

In some states, you can actually acquire a wine-only license, or a spirits-only license, so adding this to your brewery may not be difficult. Other states forbid any other alcohol other than what is made onsite in a pub…do your homework and find out what works for you.

Pros: Non-beer drinkers can enjoy your bar; brings in a new crowd; allows for mixed drinks; can feature more local products.

Cons: You will need a trained bartender, more space, larger coolers (for wine), different barware (glasses), more staff, and large amounts of money to initially start up a full bar.

Choice #4 — Owner Operator or Just Owner?

Do you want to *own* a brewpub...or do you want to *work* at a brewpub? Many people who own breweries aren't the ones that are pouring 50 pound bags of malt into the mash tun and cleaning out the kegs.

You may have a day job that you want to keep or you may have a day job you want to quit...

Whatever it is, you need to know before you start putting together your plan...especially if you have a partnership (story of that coming up)...

If you have *never* done this before, you are probably going to need some training, or at least do it on a very small scale so you can figure it out as you go along.

If you are clueless and don't *want* to have a clue, you'll need to hire a brewer and maybe a manager for the place.

Some people just think that owning a brewpub is a good business to own and they invest in one. I assume most people reading this book will actually want to work at their brewpub either as a manager or as the brewer, so most of the info will focus on those people.

Choice #5 — Sole-Proprietor or More?

Limited Liability Company (LLC), S-Corporation, Partnership, Sole-Proprietor?...your accountant would tell you this is the most important choice you'll make.

Are you doing this yourself? Are you and a few others combining to do this?

These are the questions you need to ask yourself so you can decide how to establish your company.

This isn't a, "I'll get to it later," type of thing. This is an issue that is on all of your state and federal applications. If you operate as an LLC, you need to have that DONE before you apply for your licenses.

There are advantages and disadvantages to all of the above. I went to business school long enough to say to go and ask your accountant what fits your individual needs the best.

Pros to Sole Prop: Easy to set up, no cost. Easy to close.

Cons to Sole Prop: Opens YOU up to liability.

Pros to LLC or Partnership: Covers your ass from lawsuits.

Cons to LLC or Partnership: Costs much more, adds time.

Quick Note: If you are establishing a partnership, I always stress the "work agreement". This could be, but doesn't have to be, an actual written agreement. If you are passing the idea of a brewery around to friends and you are going to go in on it, talk about RESPONSIBILITIES of each of you before you start. Who is working there, who isn't, how much money are each of you putting in, who is actually brewing the beer, what happens if someone wants out?

This is a great reality check for you and your friends.   A few simple questions now save an all out war a few months down the road. This is good advice...take it.

True Story #1: A group of four people came into my brewery a few years ago.   One of them owned a B&B, the other was some sort of professional (lawyer, maybe?), the other a cook, and the other was "an accomplished home brewer" (whatever the hell that means).

Anyway, they were going to open a brewpub at the B&B. Everyone was pretty gung-ho about it. They had equipment picked out, their space was approved, they all brewed some kick-ass beer together...all was good.

Until I asked one question...who is going to work there? They all looked at the homebrew guy. He said, "Maybe on weekends." The B&B guy said he couldn't. The lawyer was a no-go. And the cook said he'd help develop the menu but couldn't afford to leave his place of employment.

It was pretty awkward pretty quick. I figured I would change the pace and ask, "Where is your funding coming from?" In hindsight, this was an obvious mistake.

While they had made cost analysis sheets and profit/loss statements, everyone thought the lawyer was there to back it fully...except the lawyer.

He thought they'd all pitch in and get a bank loan for the construction that was leveraged against the B&B property.

This was apparently news to the property owners.

Safe to say our time together took a much different route after these questions were asked.

If you are going to have a partnership, ask these questions in your group BEFORE you get too far down the line. Get expectations in order ASAP.

Choice #6 — Rent or Own?

I say this too much for some people, but it is the most important aspect of planning your brewery: you NEED to know exactly where your brewery is located BEFORE you apply for any licenses. You can't just say "Here's my idea; I will incorporate it into whatever space I can get."

You will not get a license to do anything without an address locked up. The TTB (Tobacco Tax and Alcohol Trade Bureau) will want rental agreements, deeds and so forth with your application.

You need to decide before you start looking if you want to own your space or rent it. Over the long haul, this is probably your highest expense, so renting or owning is a big deal.

Pros to Owning – You have an asset to take out an equity loan on; you can do as you please inside/outside.

Cons to Owning – High upfront cost; when shit happens to the building YOU are going to have to fix it.

Pros to Renting – Lower upfront costs; makes it flexible if you want to move.

Cons to Renting — Owner can kick you out at any time when your lease runs out; there could be restrictions on what you can do to the building.

Extra info about renting: I don't know your situation, but I really encourage you to go for owning the space you are going to occupy. There is a world of benefits to being able to rent from yourself. Please ASK YOUR ACCOUTANT about this.

True Story #2: I'll also share a story of a brewery that was literally on the brink of closing its doors because of a rental disagreement. They had grown year after year and the owner got wind of their success...the owner then went after a HUGE rent increase giving them about 60 days notice.

They actually got to the point of posting all their equipment for sale and announcing an agreement to contract brew elsewhere while they looked for a new home or possibly close for good. In the end, an agreement was reached (for a much higher rental fee) but it was almost a disaster.

This could be you if you rent. If you are wildly successful, who's to say your landlord won't raise your rent by 50% or 100% since he knows you are growing like crazy?

Owning also gives you the flexibility of having an asset to borrow against if you ever plan an expansion or new location.

Choice #7 – Selling your beer offsite: Yes or No?

Do you plan on just selling the beer onsite, or do you plan on producing enough to go to other bars in the region?

If the answer is yes, you are going to need a larger system than someone who may just sell onsite. You'll also need kegs, a sales rep (and/or a great distributor), and storage space. This will greatly affect how large your actual brewing space and brewing systems are.

Pros to offsite sales – You get the name out more; higher sales volume; create a regional brand.

Cons to offsite sales – Lower margins; will have to brew more often; larger upfront costs.

About your choices...

Are there more than seven choices that you are going to make? Of course there are. Maybe even hundreds more. But these are seven choices that really get the gears moving. They also push you towards the first and maybe most important aspect of your brewpub...the space.

- ***Homework #2 – Think about brewpubs you have been to. What are they doing? Do they serve food? Did you like the place? Would you like to visit other places you have not been?***

What choices did I make?

You did buy a book from someone who owns and operates a brewpub, so you probably want to know what I did. I'll tell you what choices I made and why.

Choice #1 - Food yes...but not really

I operate with a 1.5 BBL system. Yep, that's it. I brew about 30-45 gallons a batch. You're probably asking yourself how I generate enough revenue to keep the doors open.

One – I do EVERYTHING myself. I brew, I sell, I bartend, I clean, I paint, I repair, I buy, I pick up, I drop off, I demolish, I fix, I serve, I prepare food, I run the webpage, I do whatever the hell needs done at the brewery. I am not paying 17 people to do these things; I do them myself, and quite honestly, I like the control of doing everything. I enjoy the owner/operator experience.

Two – I keep my costs down. When I bought the building I am currently in, it was at best a giant turd. It took MONTHS to get cleaned and repaired. But with that "sweat equity" I put in, I saved tens of thousands of dollars in acquisition costs. Also, my father-in-law is a contractor and he hooked me up with people who were good and charged a fair rate for things that I could not do.

I am also only open about 19 hours a week, so I don't need 100s of BBLs of beer on hand to serve.

With all this said, having a restaurant would be too much work. I do, however, allow people to bring in food from other restaurants. There is a pizzeria next door and probably about 20% of the patrons to the bar get the pizza and bring it over to eat.

I do have SOME food...but it is appetizer-type stuff, like a cool meat and cheese platter. It always has Sage Derby cheese on it. If you have never had Sage Derby cheese, put the book down and buy some now! And I usually make some kind of fresh salsa and chips.

I didn't want the extra staff and expense of a restaurant…and honestly, I don't need it.

Choice #2 - Beaver Brewing or bust.

I only serve my own beer onsite. It costs WAY too much in PA to add a full liquor license. I probably wouldn't do it even if I could. There is some great beer in PA, but you are coming to the *Beaver Brewing Company,* so why would I have anything else?

Choice #3 - I sell stuff other than beer.

I do Pennsylvania Wines, Meads, and Ciders at the Brewpub. I try to get the most local stuff I can.   There are some fantastic local wineries (no, not every PA wine is a super-sweet, Concord grape wine; there are other grapes in PA) and a few people make some great mead and cider, also.

In PA, you have the ability to sell all of these at no additional licensing cost.

Side Note: You'd be surprised how many people who don't like beer are dragged along with beer people to a brewery. It's not a bad idea to have at least one alternative drink.

I carry about 30 different wines and 4-5 different meads at all times. In the fall, I usually carry a cider or two. I pride myself on having just as cool a wine menu as I do beer menu.

Choice #4 - I own it AND operate myself.

Did you read #1? I am an *owner operator* and do that to keep my costs down. I didn't have $750,000 in the bank when I started this venture and didn't want to get loans to get started...that's why I operate this way (and I like it).

Now I do have an accountant, some bar staff, and other people who help with food and such but I brew all the beer myself. There are VERY FEW owner operator breweries out there but I am here to tell you it is not impossible.

Choice #5 - Sole-Proprietor.

Sole-Prop, but my lawyer is convincing me to change to LLC soon. Ask your accountant and/or lawyer what best suits your needs.

I really am a control freak when it comes down to it. I don't want other people "helping me out" throughout the process.

Again...I will reiterate...ask a lawyer or an accountant what best fits YOUR individual needs.

Choice #6 - Only one choice for me...

This was easy for me...OWN. I started renting when I opened the nanobrewery, but I knew I wanted to own my next building for a few reasons.

One, in the long run it's cheaper and you have an asset in the end. Two, I ripped the place apart and really fixed it up. No owner would have allowed a renter to do that. Three, it was a great location and great price for me.

This REALLY depends on your location. Buying may not be a viable option, but try to make it one.

Choice #7 - If you want it, go to the source...

I don't sell a drop of beer offsite.   I can't make enough to sell in-house let alone out-of-house. On top of that, it isn't all that profitable for me, so I don't do it.

So I do it with a 1.5 BBL system, but what size system do you need? That brings us to our next chapter. Well, not next, but right after this little side chapter.

- *Homework #3* **– Check out www.beaverbrewingcompany.com . (Even if you have already, do it again.) See what these choices brought to my place and see what works for you.**

Groundwork for Success

There is a whole marketing section in this book, but I'd like to go in the order of what you should do and when you should do it.

Before you even start deciding which system you want, what location to use, or when you'll tap your first Kvass (Never heard of Kvass? Look it up...), here are a few things you should really get done before moving on. There is no reason these items should not be done BEFORE you finish this book!

Get a Name

Oddly enough, your brewery *does* need a name. You may already have one, but if you don't have one picked, I want you to get one. You're going to be filling out forms and talking to potential investors. If they ask the name of the place and you say, "*I dunno,*" you're going to look like an ass.

Register Your Name

MOST states require you to fill out some sort of "business name" form.   It has a cost most places (what doesn't have a cost?), but is generally under $100.

Get a Domain Name

You've got the name, now get the web address. MOST of the people who initially came to my first location found me on the net. This also ensures that someone else won't take it. You don't have to create a site yet, but get the domain name registered; it won't cost more than $10 a year.

Sign up for all the social networking sites

Whether you like them or not, I bet your patrons are using them. Again, you don't have to send a tweet every three minutes, but get the name in your possession.

Get an agreement with your partners

This isn't a contract but it can be. I pray that you are going into business with people you know well and trust even more. Beyond a partnership agreement, I always make this suggestion.

Have a "get your shit together agreement". This is an agreement where you all sit in a room and verbally say out loud the amount of work you are putting into the project. A wrong answer in this exercise is, "Whatever needs done." A right answer is, "Fill out all the forms, work the bar four nights a week, and do all the accounting."

Specifically outline what you are going to do OUT LOUD. You may find there is someone in your group who only wants to invest money and never wants to work at the brewery. Others may assume they are going to work their asses off at the place but put up none of their own money.

It's a great idea to know this BEFORE you start planning.

Again, read the example I gave earlier about people coming in who had ZERO idea of what each other was going to do for their project.

Tell Your Significant Other

Can't tell you how many times I have heard someone say, *"Don't know what my wife is going to think about this."* (Women always tell their husbands, but frequently the husbands don't tell the wives.) I don't need to go into why this should be done.

Explain your plan to a family member

Who knows you better? Probably no one better than your family. They don't have to agree with your plan and that's not a bad thing. But they do know you better than just about anyone, so they may have some great advice.

What size brewing system do I need?

This is the *second* most dreaded question I get when I do consulting sessions with future brewers. Because the answer every single time is, "I don't know". How much beer do you want to sell...how much do you *NEED* to sell to cover your costs.

This pains me, but I have to use some math here; to be honest, a whole hell of a lot of math.

I am going to show you what you can expect in output in terms of beer with various sizes of systems that ACTUAL brewpubs use. I only go up to 10 BBL systems...if you are planning on doing a 20+ BBL system, you wouldn't be reading this book, you would be reading one about starting a production brewery. By the way, **BBL** stands for **Barrel of Beer** which is 31 U.S. Gallons.

The goal of this section is to predetermine what size system you want or need. After we go through the financial section, please come back and see what you NEED to have.

I am already imagining the emails I will get from this next section... "These numbers are stupid; I think it should be this, or you went too high on that." Well, if that's what you think, then by all means change the numbers.

I do, however, provide a simple formula for you to determine how much beer can be made on each system, and how many pints you get out of each system on an annual basis. If you think I estimated too high or too low with a number, plug in your own damn numbers. My feelings will not be hurt.

There are some scary charts coming up with a whole bunch of numbers that I am sure will scare the hell out of you. Let's start with chart 1.1:

	Fermenters			
Size Brewhouse	1	2	3	4
1 BBL	36	73	109	146
2 BBL	73	146	219	292
3 BBL	109	218	327	436
5 BBL	182	364	546	728
7 BBL	255	510	765	1020
10 BBL	365	730	1095	1460

(figure 1.1: Annual BBL production)

This chart shows your annual BBL production based on the number of fermenters you have. It also assumes each beer stays in the fermenter for ten days (meaning you can use it 36.5 times a year) then it is immediately moved to condition elsewhere (bottles, kegs, brite tanks, etc.) and that those spaces are unlimited. It also assumes the fermenters are the same size as your system (I.E. 3BBL system and 3 BBL fermenters). The numbers are also rounded down.

Now that you have the BBLs, you know how many pints you have to serve. A pint is 16 ounces. However, many bars serve in 12 ounce or even 14 ounce glasses. They also serve in 8 ounce snifters, or beer samples at 4 to 5 ounces a drink. The next chart shows how many *16 ounce pours* you get based on your system size and amount of fermenters. This takes into account growler sales, samplers, etc.

To generate the next chart we use this simple formula:

There are 40 pints in a 5 gallon sixtel keg and 240 pints in a BBL of beer. Multiply the BBLs of beer you make annually by 240...that will give you your pint production by the year. Here's a breakdown:

Size Brewhouse	Pints Annually			
	1	2	3	4
1 BBL	8640	17520	26160	35040
2 BBL	17520	35040	52560	70080
3 BBL	26160	52320	78480	104640
5 BBL	43680	87360	131040	174720
7 BBL	61200	122400	183600	244800
10 BBL	87600	175200	262800	350400

(figure 1.2: Annual Pint Production)

So looking at this chart, you can see that if you had a 3 BBL brew house, brewed 36.5 times a year, and had 2 fermenters, you could produce 52,320 pints of beer a year. Sounds like a lot...but it really isn't if you consider this:

Let's say the average patron drinks 2 pints. At some places, patrons drink more than that (at my brewpub it's higher, but this is a good baseline...the more food you have the lower the number, the less the higher, in general) and some are less, but let's keep things simple.

Let's also assume you are open just 4 days a week, or 208 days a year. To sell those 52,320 pints, you would need to sell 252 pints each day. At 2 pints per patron, you would need to serve 126 patrons a day in order to sell every drop of beer you produced:

$$(52,320/208) / 2 = 126$$

OR

(Annual Pints / Days Open a Year) / Pints per person = Patrons needed each day

Think you'll be open 6 days a week? Think you can squeeze 2.25 pints out of each patron? Then just plug in the numbers to the formula I just outlined to give you the number of customers you would need daily to serve all of that beer:

$$(52,320/312) / 2.5 = 67$$

You can also work the formula backwards. For example, if you think you will only get 50 patrons a day, and be open only 3 days a week, and they will drink 2 pints per visit, then how many pints would you need a year?

50 patrons x 2 pints x 156 days = 15,200 pints needed

You could get away with having a 1 BBL system and just 2 fermenters to meet the demand.

I cannot stress enough that the formulas work! Please - you can fudge the numbers a bit...assuming you get more patrons, less keg efficiency, whatever, please change the numbers. But keep the formula; it will tell you what size system you want or NEED to get.

Please refer back to this after we go over your financials. You may find that you need a much larger system to cover your costs.

Also, note that *this is only for serving people onsite*. It doesn't take into account that you may sell your beer in kegs to bars offsite.

I always recommend that you try selling all of your beer onsite because it is the most profitable.

However, there are MANY pubs that sell offsite, so if that is for you, please calculate how large of a system you will need. The formula can be tweaked to add keg sales into the mix.

I will say this, and initially it won't make too much sense: Your size system really depends on the costs of your business.

While on the surface that may sound crazy, consider this: If you are in downtown New York City, you will need a MUCH larger system than if you are in downtown Beaver Falls. Your costs are much higher in NYC, and that will mean you'll need a larger system. Take this into account when you're planning.

- ***Homework #4 – Crunch some numbers to get a rough idea of the size system you will need. Can you go nano or do you have to go big?***

Brewer's note: I find that the average customer drinks about 3 glasses per visit. Quite a few people drink samplers and that alone is 1.5 beers. They usually grab a pint after that.

Finding Space

So, now that you know how large of a system you will want, (not *need* because we don't know your costs yet) you can start looking for space. Now, I know from my consulting that you really want to start filling out paperwork right now…

STOP. You can't fill out any paper work until you have a location. On most forms this is the very first question, *"What is your brewery's physical location?"*

This is the MOST IMPORTANT AND TIME CONSUMING PHASE of opening a brewery. You're thinking to yourself that you already have a space and you can skip this chapter....don't. Just having the space isn't enough. There are plenty of ducks you need to get in a row before that "space" becomes a brewpub.

'Location, Location, Location...'

I am sure you have heard the saying, that these are the three most important words in real estate...

I am here to tell you that is not the case for brewpubs. Let's take a look at where a few are located.

First Up — Sprague Farm and Brew Works:

Address: 22113 US HWY 6 & 19, Box H, Venango, PA 16440

Population of Venango, PA, is 288.

I myself have been inside the pub on several occasions. Rarely have I NOT stood in line for at least a minute or two waiting for a beer...not because of service, but because the place is packed.

I'd like you to bring up an online map of the address that is written down here...there is NOTHING around this bar. And that is not an exaggeration.

If you think this is a small farm town near Pittsburgh or Philly and that's where all the people come from, you are wrong. The total population of Crawford County (where Venango is located) is around 89,000, and the closest "city" is Erie, PA, about a 30 minute drive from the pub.

It is LITERALLY ON A FARM! Not your typical location for a brewpub, but this place has been up and running for years and shows no signs of slowing down.

What does this show? It shows that if you have a cool place, good beer, and friendly staff, you can make your pub work in a very small town.

Many restaurant start-up books will state that you can expect around 90% of your patrons to come from a 3-5 mile radius of your place.

While you may be operating a restaurant, you are also operating a brewery...there probably are not 35 breweries in a 10 mile radius of you, so naturally you will draw from a larger area since there are no other closer choices for people in your region.

Beaver Brewing Company:

Address: 1820 7th Ave, Beaver Falls, PA 15010

Population of Beaver Falls is 8,987. Population of Beaver County is 170,539.

The brewery is located on the main street of downtown Beaver Falls.   Now you may say, "Hey, he's in a college town, that's why it works."   I would tell you it doesn't matter. Geneva College is less than a mile away, but the college is founded on the principles of Reformed Presbyterians…i.e. they are not big on drinking beer.

I am, however, located on a busy state route, near a turnpike exit, and near another 10-15 small towns. I'm also about 45 minutes outside of Pittsburgh and many patrons of the bar come from the suburbs of Pittsburgh, a handful from the actual city.

I would say Beaver Falls is your typical "small town USA". Lots of family-run businesses in town and most people who live there grew up within 5-10 miles of the town.

There is MUCH more traffic that goes past Beaver Brewing on a daily basis than at Sprague Farms Brewery, but both have their followings and the places are filled.

Southern Tier Brewing Company™:

Address: 2072 Stoneman Circle, Lakewood, NY 14750

Population of Lakewood, NY: 3,258 Population of Chautauqua County is 134,905.

I'm sure you have heard of the legendary *"Pumpking"*. Their pumpkin beer is one of the more sought after beers in the craft market.

They also operate a pub, "The Empty Pint," that is attached to their brewery. I have been going there for years (even when the brewery was across the street in an industrial /business park), and the place is packed in the summer, fall, winter, and spring.

Lakewood, NY, is a tourist-type town. It has a 4-month season.   Chautauqua Lake is about one mile from the pub and attracts many people throughout the summer. However, the pub is ALWAYS packed with people. It is also off the beaten path near a business park.

This is an example of a brewpub located in a seasonal area that attracts people 12 months a year to their pub. They don't have thousands of people driving by each day (maybe not even 100) but still manage to stay busy.

So why did I pick these three examples?

They just show that you don't have to be in Times Square to attract customers. Don't think you have to have the best location with the most eyeballs driving past daily.

While that doesn't hurt, it does cost more money. If you have the money, please locate in the coolest, most visible part of your community. What I am here to tell you is that if you can't, you still can be very successful.

General Items to look for when scoping out locations...

The building may be cool, the location great, but nothing else works. Please take a mile-high view of the potential brewing space. Make sure it actually WORKS before you sign the mortgage/lease agreement. Here are some items to consider to help you choose the perfect space.

1. **Zoning**

This could be 1, 2, 3, 4, and 5. It could shut down your dreams of the "perfect spot" before they start. Breweries are categorized as "Light Industrial" in terms of zoning.

This could be 1, 2, 3, 4, and 5. It could shut down your dreams of the "perfect spot" before they start. Breweries are categorized as "Light Industrial" in terms of zoning.

NOT A MISPRINT – I put this in here twice because it is that *important* to know.

More than likely your town does not have any classification for brewpubs in its zoning ordinance. These are new and small in number, so they are rarely defined in any local zoning ordinances and nothing so far in the international building codes mention brewpubs.

I will talk generally about what you should look for in terms of zoning, variances, and use changes, but I beg of you...**please call your local zoning officer**...explain what you want to do, ask where it could be possible in your town, and what you would need to do to open a pub.

In some towns, there are no zoning ordinances. I know of a few breweries that have opened on their own property. Others take 2+ years to open because they have issues with building codes and zoning. I am going to go step-by-step over the process I went through and this should help.

HOWEVER – YOUR EXPERIENCE WILL BE DIFFERENT! Every town/county/state has its own zoning ordinances and some interpret codes differently than others.

True Story #3 First, the story of my first location where I just had a brewery. The space was a pizza shop before I moved in. It was a commercially zoned building, but I am a light manufacturer, not allowed in commercial buildings.

The space was perfect, so I had to make it work. The area, Patterson Township, actually wanted me there, so they wanted it to work. They told me if I could get an engineer or architect to say my use is similar to the previous use in the building, everything would be cool.

Luckily, I convinced an architect that making pizza and selling it retail was "similar" to making beer and selling it for "take-out" growlers. It worked for town council and two months later I was brewing beer.

This is possibly the luckiest scenario that could have happened. The town was cool with it, the architect was, too, and everything LUCKILY fell into place.

Take Away From the Story:

Can you say your use is similar to the previous use of the building? If it was a restaurant you may have a chance. I know that several brewpubs are classified as restaurants by their local zoning officer and that saves a host of problems.

Now with my brewpub, things were MUCH different.

I did it backwards. I fell in love with a building and just bought it. The deal was amazing and there was a tenant in there already. Worst case scenario for me was that I buy the building, the city turns my application down, and I rent it out for a profit. Not a bad deal at the time.

So after I bought the building, I told the city my intentions and what I wanted to do. THE EASY WAY would have been for them to say the pub is classified as a restaurant and you can move into our commercial district easily….they didn't. Their zoning law clearly states that if the use isn't clearly stated (brewpubs were not mentioned) in the zoning code for that area, you need a variance.

In short, I would try and argue that you are operating a restaurant, it just happens to be that I would also be "cooking" your drinks there too.

On with my story...My chances of getting a variance were slim; by slim I mean none. The way the laws were written, it would have been nearly impossible. By another stroke of luck (and having a knowledgeable attorney) I got the variance on a technicality.

I submitted my application when I knew they didn't have a quorum for the zoning hearing board. They couldn't hear the case for over 60 days, and state law says if the board doesn't act upon an application within 60 days, it is deemed as passed.

Take Away from This Story:

One, God loves me. I am one of the luckiest people in the world. I always win when I go to a casino, my wife is beautiful, and I have great friends and family.

Second, get legal advice if you need a variance or conditional use. Find someone who is an expert in municipal law; there are plenty out there. Luckily, my brother-in-law is one of the best municipal law experts in the region and guided me through the process. If it wasn't for him, I would have gone to the zoning hearing board and been rejected.

Again, every town is COMPLETELY different. This is just one story of what it took to get a variance. Some towns may not even require one at all depending on where you locate.

I know of several people who had signed leases for spaces and were turned down by their city council because they couldn't meet the town's regulations. I met one brewer who actually bought a building and waited 25 months to start brewing there because of a zoning issue.

Moral of the story: CALL YOUR LOCAL ZONING OFFICER IF YOU ARE LOOKING FOR SPACE IN A SPECIFIC AREA. This will save you months and possibly years of time and headaches.

But hey, I'm just one guy...how important could this really be? I should ask someone else...

Well, look no further. One of my best friends growing up and my college roommate, Kasey Turner, had to one-up me and start his own *production* brewery.

He and the other owner, Justin Bonner (who dreamed of being a pimp before he got into beer), shared their insight on zoning and I am sharing it with you here. They are the principles at *Jailbreak Brewing Company*.

"Zoning was a key issue for us. We were looking at locations in two counties—one that already had zoning to permit production breweries and one that had proposed zoning to do so. The county that was proposing zoning has two industrial zones—heavy and light.

They were going to permit breweries brewing up to 10,000 BBLs per year into light zoning and anything over 10,000 BBLs would need to be in heavy industrial zones. The real problem for us was that this zoning was attached to a "comprehensive rezoning" bill that contained every zoning change in the county.

As one would imagine, many were routine requests but some generated much negative feedback. That county was our preferred location, so we contacted the county executive's office to set up a meeting.

We were told that the vote was scheduled for sometime over the summer, but because of the amount of community involvement and interest, that it might be pushed to September to allow for more public hearings. This would delay our start by at least 3-4 months, which was unacceptable to us.

We, via the county executive's office, had several other meetings with the county. We established our credibility by showing our financial projections, by demonstrating that we had no debt and quite a bit of our own money put up to start the business, and by hiring a professional brewer with decades of experience (as opposed to being a couple of homebrewers trying to go pro).

When the county saw that and saw that they were in a competition for our business, they moved to separate the brewery zoning from the comprehensive rezoning. We spoke with one county councilman and gave the same set of background information to him to appease any concerns he might have had.

After a couple of council meetings to properly separate the brewery zoning, we had our vote and it passed unanimously. We are now poised to be the first production brewery in the county's history."

Great story of how much planning and work goes into this BEFORE you even start thinking about making beer. I know it was a little different (they weren't doing a pub) but the story is interchangeable.

Homework #5: Check out JailbreakBrewing.com. They run a nice blog and if you read it in a timeline starting at the beginning, you will see a nice story of their opening unfold.

2. Building Codes

So you have the ability to do what you want to do in the building you want to do it in...Now comes in some inspector saying you have to make all of these changes to the building before you can open.

It is worth your while to ask an architect or engineer who is familiar with commercial building codes to do a walk-through of the building before you purchase it or sign a lease.

In many areas, when you change the use of a building, you have to update the entire building with the International Uniform Construction Code. If you are purchasing an old building, this could be a nightmare (like it was for me).

I had to add a fire escape, which doesn't sound like much, but it was. The design of the building made me have to knock out a brick wall, add a hallway, and add a set of stairs going out the back. That wasn't cheap.

I also had to add insulation, plumbing, new doors, a fire safety system, a carbon monoxide alarm system, lighting, exhaust fans, signage, new electrical outlets everywhere, specialized sinks; demo walls; and address handicap accessibility issues , plus a few hundred other items to get it up to code.

3. Space

Just how big is your actual place in terms of square footage? How much do you need?

Some states have requirements on how large your serving area has to be. (In PA it is 300 square feet.) And don't forget, you are also going to be brewing there, and people will be eating, and going to the bathroom, etc. A small storefront downtown may be cool, but it may not be large enough for you.

I really recommend using an architect to tell you what you can fit into your desired space.

Let the architect know what the state requires before a work crew gets started so you have a solid plan.

Note: Many states and towns actually **require drawings** with the submittal of your application for a brewery or zoning changes. But since you have already called your local zoning officer, you already know what is required...

Brewer's Note: So how big is the Beaver Brewing Company? The upstairs bar area, bathrooms, seating, and all other public space is about 2,700 sq ft. The brewing area (much of which is not used since I am nano-sized) is about 3,100 sq ft. Plenty of room for the pending expansion! There are also 15 foot ceilings on each floor, so moving in equipment is never an issue.

4. Utilities and Quality of Space

Here is something not to overlook...can you actually brew there? Is there natural gas, enough electric, does the place have a basement?

You can't brew with a 7 BBL system on the 3rd floor of a wood-framed building.   Having a basement helps. Having one with a loading dock helps even more.

There are some other things people often overlook:

- Generally, you want people there. Unless they are all walking to your pub, you'll need ample parking.
- Can you get deliveries there? You'll be getting equipment, grain, and other fun stuff at your place; is the area able to handle a tractor trailer outside to deliver your items?
- How's the roof? You're not making cheese there, you're making beer. If you have a leaky roof you'll also have mold. Check the walls, the roof, everything you can get your eyes on, and check for water damage. If there is water damage there is mold…take it from someone who worked at a mold remediation company for three years; it can be a mess.
- Can I install an exhaust fan? Some towns are very anal about where you can install exhaust fans for your kitchen/brewery. And, if you are cooking, you NEED one. This shouldn't be an issue in most areas, but it is worth looking into. Could be a headache down the road.

Brewer's note: I use all on-street parking since I am in a downtown area, but you may find that you need to add parking. I also have a loading dock (that has been used MANY times) and I had the roof repaired *BEFORE* I opened.

5. Things I don't want you to focus on...

Color - You can always paint walls or change the flooring at a minimal expense.

Layout - Unless it is a load-bearing wall, you can take it out. Don't panic if the floor plan isn't perfect when you move in.

Bathrooms - A real estate agent once told me bathrooms are the ultimate deal breaker in commercial building purchases. It didn't make sense to me or him but he swears by it. If you hate the bathrooms, remember that they are very easy to remodel.

Pretty much, if it can be changed, don't fret over it. Now, if it CAN'T be changed, you'll need to start planning alternative routes to get what you need.

Public Meetings

This book is set up as a timeline (I hope you have realized that by now.). You have your groundwork down ...you have your system, your proposed location, and now you need to get approval to do what you want to do there.

I worked in politics for over six years and have made over several hundred presentations at municipal meetings, so I consider myself an expert in working with local government.

I've spent countless hours trying to stay awake as I waited my turn to speak. I'm about to pour all of that knowledge into this book and hopefully *you* remain awake.

I beg of you, read this section. Many of you will skip it, thinking to yourself, "Hey, I want to open a brewery. I don't need a civics lesson!" I am here to tell you that you do. I have consulted with dozens of people opening a brewery and only one did not have to make *at least one* presentation to the local government.

More than likely, you will need to attend *AT LEAST* one meeting with your local town council. It may be with the planning commission, the zoning hearing board, or town council. This will prep you for what to expect.

This is another portion of the book I am sure some a-hole will email me about and say "Geez, that's common sense; I already knew that." Well, quite honestly MOST people have never made a presentation to a local town council...beyond that, MOST people have never made any type of public presentation at all.

If you fall into either of these categories...PAY ATTENTION! All the hard work you poured into finding the space could be washed away if you fail here.

Here are some tips that will make your life easier and give you a much better chance of getting your idea/project passed.

Do your Homework – Whether you are coming in to get a variance or a plan approved, whatever, read the local code book before you go to the meeting. This will make your life much easier.

Bring Supporting Documents – Sounds obvious, but I've seen dozens of people come into a public meeting with nothing more than their own words. If you have a site picked out (and you should), bring pics of the OUTSIDE AND INSIDE of the place. Some people on the board may not know what building you are talking about. Also bring any site plans you have. Those will help tell your story.

Plus, some people won't listen to you at all; they will just stare at whatever you bring...take it from me, this is true and happens more than you think.

Bring Supporters – Do the neighbors of your brewpub support the plan? If so, bring them along. You can also get signatures of people within 100 yards of the premises showing you asked them about your plan and they support it. Remember, these people are elected or appointed to their positions; an easy way to lose their seats is by supporting a project everyone in the community hates. If they know locals support the idea, it is a major feather in their caps.

Be Polite – Most human beings are nice, understanding people. However, when some of these humans get behind a podium with their name on it they can get a little crazy. If they start asking crazy questions, answer them politely; there is no winning with these people so there is no reason to get them angry.

Seems like a no-brainer, but I have heard these words from a board member, "You're pissing me off so I'm voting NO, no matter what you are proposing."

Know Your Shit – Don't come to a meeting unprepared. Bring statistics, have timelines, find similar towns that have supported similar projects. The more of an "expert" you look like, the more confidence people have in you and, therefore, your project.   Also be prepared for questions…

Common Public Meeting Questions

They aren't going to ask you what temperature you mash your IPA at or what yeast strain is your favorite, so don't worry about that right now.

More than likely, the people sitting in front of you have no idea there is a craft beer boom.

Don't believe me? Take a look at the market-share for the "Big 3" brewers. Their major concerns are the impact on the community. Here are some common public meeting questions and some good answers for them.

I recommend you read this section before your first meeting and craft your own answers.

Keep in mind these are PUBLIC meetings, so the public can come in and ask these questions even if the board doesn't.

"What are you going to do about the smell?"

Guaranteed this gets asked at least once. If you open a pub and this doesn't get asked, please stop in and I am buying you your first beer. I always like the response of "Do you like the smell of fresh baked bread? Well, those are the same ingredients I am using, so the smell isn't necessarily *bad*."

I'd also have a plan for your spent grains. If you say, "We are going to toss them in the alley for a few months," there will be problems. This is a make-or-break item for some people, so be prepared.

"We don't need another bar."

Not really a question, but this is a common concern. You must explain you are not another "bar". You are a manufacturer and you are serving a product made at your facility in-house.

I've been to bars where there is more puke on the walls of the bathroom than paint. Craft beer brewpubs are not the places where people get shitfaced and disrupt the entire town. Bring some info on the pricing of your beer and that this will bring people with disposable income into the community and support the other businesses. It also won't detract from other bars since yours is a specialty item.

"How many people will work there?"

Whether you're Mitt Romney, Barack Obama, or Mr. Mayor, you are always campaigning on "jobs created" in your town. They can't hold you to this, but give them a range of people that will work there. Also let them know you plan on being successful and expanding in their town if the project is approved.

"How late will you be open? Will there be noise?"

These questions are usually combined. You may be in a residential area and noise could be an issue. If you are, take the initiative and say something like, "All our bands will stop playing music by 10 pm," or, "We aren't going to have outdoor seating. "

You also need an idea of your operating hours. You may be closing up at 9 pm; if you are, let them know; or you may be closing at 2 am, that matters, too. Whatever it is, make sure they know and assure them you will make the place safe.

"When is this going to happen? How long will it take?"

Have a timeline; this makes you look prepared.

"What about parking?"

Show me a town that doesn't panic about parking and I'll show you my pet unicorn. This is doubly important if only street parking is available for your place. Find out the ordinances for parking in your zoning district. Make sure you can meet those demands (or come damn close).

If you are building a parking lot, let them know how many spaces, and what type of lot. You'd be surprised, but a gravel lot will get you a bunch of frowns. These are dusty and can be a major issue with your neighbors.

Best advice I can give is BE PREPARED for these meetings. I've said it several times but it is important. I have seen so many people crash and burn at these things, not because their plans weren't any good, but because they weren't prepared.

"What about under-age drinking?"

Honestly, this is a common question I have come across. It's almost absurd to answer, but prepare for it. I like two answers for this one:

First, my pricing is an immediate deterrent. No 16-year-olds are dropping $7.00 on an 8 ounce snifter of barley wine at your pub. They are buying a $5 gallon jug of vodka to split with their friends.

Second, this is your livelihood. You are not risking your license to make $5 off of an under-age drinker.

Start looking like you actually own a business

Would you buy a wedding ring from a guy hanging out on a sidewalk wearing Zubaz® pants and a flannel shirt? No.

As a matter of fact, you wouldn't even listen to him.

People won't listen to *you* if you don't act the part.

The following are two VERY easy and inexpensive things to do.

One: Get a REAL email that identifies you and your company.

Of the following two emails addresses, which do you think a bank manager or potential business partner would answer first?

DanTheBrewMaster1981@hotmail.com

OR

Dan@beaverbrewingcompany.com

If you said the second one you are correct. Get a domain and get email for it.

Two: Get business cards

Not ones you printed at home; get real ones. They cost about $10 and make you look like you know what you are doing and that you are serious.

People immediately respect what you are doing if you have these.   If you don't, it will send up some red flags to the wrong people. Trust me.

By the way, the second one is my REAL email address. Feel free to drop me a line some time.

Finances

My most dreaded section of the book. I hate writing this for a few reasons. So here's a little introduction before we start...

One, I give honest advice. People hate that. If you hate honesty, skip this section.

You WILL HAVE TO DO SOME WORK to open your brewery.

First, going through financial info is one of those steps. I can't do it for you. Only you know how much money you have to invest. I can't lay it out for you that you need exactly $235,984.47 to open your brewpub because EVERY situation is different.

Secondly, people ask the STUPIDEST questions when it comes to money. You may have heard there are no stupid questions; I am here to tell you that information is incorrect.

One of my favorite questions is, *"I'm planning on opening a brewery in XXX city. Do you think I can afford to do that with a 2 BBL system?"*

How in the hell would I know? Seriously, I got two sentences of information! We will get into why I have no clue in a bit...

Third. I have to repeat this sentence over, and over, and over. *"If you don't know the costs of setting up your brewery, I can't tell you what to charge for your beer."* I think people can sense how much I loathe the following questions:

"What type of margins will I need on my beer sales?" or "How much should I charge?"

Generally, I force a very fake smile and shake my head with the answer, "I don't know." And I can't know unless you know your costs.

By the end of this section you will have the tools to actually determine how to price out your beer! It takes A LOT of time on your part because YOU HAVE TO DO ONE IMPORTANT STEP, which brings me to the most important aspect of this section...maybe the book.

KNOW THE COSTS OF YOUR BUSINESS INSIDE AND OUT

It is imperative that you know how much this is going to cost you. If your startup costs are $1,000,000, you better sell a whole hell of a lot of beer. If they are $50,000, you better be ready to work your ass off because you don't have the money to have other people do the work for you.

Some General Terms You Should Know...

Honestly, I really didn't want to add this section to the book because it seemed a little like filler to me, but I have talked to enough people to know there will be MANY of you reading this that don't know these terms.

Sure, they shake their heads, raise an eyebrow, and repeatedly say, "Yes, I know," but really they are clueless.

Some are beer related, some business related. If you know these, great for you; if you don't, you're welcome.

We aren't all finance wizards who went to business school. MOST of you will think you know the terms, but please, take the time and refresh your memory. You don't want to be embarrassed at the bank loan meeting.

These are words that investors may throw around while talking to you. Instead of nodding your head and acting like you know it...why not just know it?

All of these are written for humans to understand, not dictionary definitions:

Revenue: Money that people pay you for your beer. The more beer you sell...the more revenue you get.   REVENUE IS NOT PROFIT.

Overhead Costs: In general, these are costs that you will incur whether you make one damn beer or not. Think mortgage/rent, property taxes, salaried staff, etc.

Variable Costs: These are costs that change depending on how much product you make...the more beer you make, the more you spend. Think materials like malt, yeast, hops.

Profit: Revenue – Expenses (costs) = Profit. Profit is also NOT net revenue.

Net Revenue: Revenue – Discounts. Did you have a 10% off coupon or some other "deal"? If you did, this is your net revenue.

Working Capital: Current Assets – Current Liabilities = Working Capital. An easy way to look at this would be to take what you own (cash, accounts receivable, inventory) and subtract what you owe, like debt, accounts receivable, etc. Another description would be all the money or assets you can use NOW.

Are there more things you should know? Probably there are, but this info makes you smarter than about 98% of the population, so you are headed in the right direction.

Determining Your Costs

Again, this takes some work. Well, that's a lie....honestly it takes *a lot of work*. If you complete this task in less than five minutes, you did something wrong.

Now, why do I drill the idea of KNOWING YOUR COSTS into your brain? Because you can't know what to charge for your beer unless you know your costs inside and out.

Remember that term, "profit"? It is revenue minus your expenses.   If you don't know your expenses, you will never know how much money you are making...and neither will anyone investing in your project, so they probably WON'T INVEST in your project unless they know what you are getting into.

So how do you figure out what your costs will be?

Let's break it down two ways...

First: Start-up Costs

These are costs you will incur before making one drop of beer. I have included a list below that should provide you with a STARTING POINT for determining your costs. Yours will be and should be different, but this is a start.   These are generally overhead costs and most are sunk costs.

Gotcha! Sunk cost was not in the definition section, but this proves a point that people will mention terms you aren't familiar with. Don't panic; many people run successful businesses and have no idea what these fancy words are.

In case you didn't know, *sunk costs* are costs that you have incurred, and you are never seeing again. An example would be this book...you paid for it and it may or may not be useful to you. It doesn't really matter anymore because your money is already gone.

Back to the more important matters...

I'll start with broad categories and I'll break it down after that.

- Equipment: Fermenters, Boilers, Tubes, Hoses, Heat Exchanger, etc.
- Kegs
- Rent/Mortgage, Property Taxes
- Renovation Costs: Painting, Demo, Architect/Engineer, Contractor, build-out
- Licensing/Permits: Occupancy Permit, Building Permit, Brewery License
- Insurance: Property, Liability, Workman's Comp
- Furniture: Tables, Chairs, Bar, etc.
- Kitchen (optional): Hoods, Fryers, prep areas, cold rooms, etc.

Add all these up and you have your general start-up costs. I would recommend you do this on a spreadsheet. Don't panic if the numbers change over time; they should once you learn more.

Note:

If you haven't done this already, please start right away. Create a spreadsheet with all of your costs. List all of the items/services you plan on incurring and put cost estimates along with them.

In the end, you will have a number that will let you know how much money you need to start. I have dozens of spreadsheets I have made over the past few years helping me budget out costs. These were EXTREMELY helpful to me.

Second: Variable or Operational Costs

You start incurring operational costs once you actually start making beer and selling your product. These include the following examples:

- Utilities: Water, Gas, Electric, Garbage, Internet, Phone, Cable, Sewer
- Staff: Brewer, Servers, Accountant, Lawyers, etc.
- Beer Materials: Malt, Yeast, Hops
- Taxes: Sales/Excise Tax
- Food (optional): Ingredients

Again, create a spreadsheet with all of these categories and start plugging in numbers. Now, I know your next question...where do I get the numbers?

This is the hard- work section I told you about. You will need quotes on materials (which you can call and get), quotes on utilities (which you can call and get), quotes on building expenses (which you can call and get).

We are getting very close to determining how much to sell your beer for, so please be patient. I will draw out a hypothetical scenario so you'll know how to do this yourself.

I like to break things down monthly since most bills are paid monthly, but understand some are paid up front.

You have determined all of your costs and know what your material/variable costs are for everything.

You spent $100,000 on equipment, and your renovation of the building was $40,000. You have also determined that your licensing, architect, and all other start-up fees are an additional $100,000. You are looking at a total start-up cost of $240,000 and you are planning on paying for all of those expenses this year.

You have a 5 BBL system and plan on brewing once a week, every single week. This will give you about 80,000 servings a year (give or take). In terms of materials for the beer, you are spending $50,000. Your staff, taxes, and utilities are roughly another $100,000.

Altogether, you have an annual expense of about $390,000. If you have 80,000 servings of beer, how much would you have to charge to break even? (Break even is having your costs equal to your revenue.)

Take your annual expenses ($390,000) and divide that by your servings (80,000) and that will give you $4.875 to charge per serving to break even.

This is a very reasonable price for a pint of beer in today's market. Over time, some of these costs go away (you don't pay an architect every year or a contractor to build the building each year) and that will add to your profit. Some costs come up that aren't here, like training, travel expenses, new equipment, replacing furniture, etc.

This will, however, give you a sanity check. In this scenario, if your expenses were $1,000,000 you would have to charge $12.50 a pint to break even in year one...that ain't happening.

You can now see just how critical this step is. You can easily get an idea of how much you need to spend, how many people you need in the door, and what you NEED to price your beer at to make money.

Some people make very complex spreadsheets pricing each item to the penny and that is fine and dandy. If that is what you want to do, please go right ahead. While it isn't a bad idea, don't get so wrapped up in the numbers you don't focus on everything else.   I have seen people spend 7 to 12 months on this step…that is too much time.

Get a ballpark number. Are you comfortable with it? Can you make enough profit for you to live your life? Only you can answer that, but if you don't know your costs you will never know!

Side Note on Music…

A little FYI for you on playing music in your place…if you don't want to do this, feel free to move on. But just so you know…You can't just flip on the radio in your bar for "free".

Those people who perform that music actually like to get paid for it. And since you are entertaining people in a public setting, you have to pay those performers.

Without going into gory details, you need to pay for the ability to play music. Even if you have live bands that cover other bands, YOU need to pay.

There are tons of ways to do this. You will get sued if you don't. It happens all the time, so take my advice and do your homework. Now back to beer…

Raising Money and the Business Plan

My brewery and brewpub are totally self-funded. I didn't take loans from a bank, or raise money from investors. There was no internet campaign...nothing.

I don't like appeasing other people, and if you take their money you are going to have to do just that.

While I did go to one of the best business schools around (University of Pittsburgh), I didn't create a business plan. To me it was a complete waste of time. The only reason you really need one is if you are going around and asking for money. If you go that route, you almost have to have SOMETHING written down.

If you need to raise cash here are some tips that will help you get ahead:

1. How much skin do YOU have in the game?

When I worked in economic development/politics I can tell you nothing aggravated me more than someone coming in, laying out a plan, claiming to hire 100 people in our area, and all that was needed was $20,000,000. The number was fine, but when we asked, "How much are YOU investing, some would look back and say, "Nothing".

I want you to do an exercise. Say the next sentence out loud:

"I want you to give me money for a project I am not willing to put a dime of my own money into."

You probably chuckled to yourself since it sounds just that stupid.

You have to invest something. If not, prepare to be in the raising money phase for a long time.

2. Know your shit

"Well, thanks for the tip," is probably going through your mind right now. This seems way too obvious. However, MANY people pitch their idea without knowing answers to MANY questions people have about their project.

Know your costs, your revenue projections, your location, and your theme before you even casually talk to investors about your project.

Sure, you can tell them your beer is awesome, but if they are shelling out a few hundred grand, they will want to know how you plan on turning that into *more* cash.

If you don't know it inside and out, you will look unprepared and you will remain unfunded.

3. Don't rely on banks for 100% of the funding

This goes back to point #1. Unless you have some serious collateral (a paid-off house, trust fund, guaranteed income) banks aren't going to fund 100% of your project. Don't do all of this planning and then just think you will get a loan because you have a great idea. It doesn't work that way.

4. Be comfortable with the terms

Don't sign a deal just because it is a deal. I have been offered money to expand five times so far. None of the deals worked for me. I wasn't comfortable giving up parts of my business or allowing people to dictate how I would expand.

Sure, I'd probably be making a few extra bucks, but I'd be miserable if I did.

5. Have a growth strategy

If an investor makes $10,000 in year one, he wants to make $15,000 in year two, and $25,000 the third, and so on and so on. Have a growth plan laid out that shows him he will be making more money each year if all goes as planned.

6. Get creative

There are dozens of breweries out there that have generated funds in unique ways like internet campaigns, selling "stock" in their company, and other wacky ideas.

This may be the route with you. Don't get stuck on going to a bank to get the money; get creative.

Tips for the Business Plan

While I am not a huge fan of business plans, it doesn't mean they have no value.   The next few words of wisdom also apply to creating your financial spreadsheet, so don't skip it to save 30 seconds...

1.   Just the Facts

No one needs the fluff about how this is a lifelong dream of yours and you will be pouring your heart into it. Stick with your PLAN as well as how much you are going to be making in terms of profit.

2.   Use something other than words

You know why the NFL™ is so damn popular? Because it is one game a week per team...People have some REALLY short attention spans and reading really stretches the limits for most of them. Show graphs, charts, pictures...anything to break up the words.

3.   Use REAL numbers

What are your projections made from, thin air? I hope not. KNOW YOUR COSTS and conservatively estimate your revenue.

4. Don't type "Business Plan Template" into google.com and fill in the blanks

This looks cheap and like you didn't put in much effort. I would compare this to the mistake of using a resume template...they look like templates...don't use them.

5. Projections

Have at least three years of projections for revenue and costs. Five years are ideal, but you need at least three.

Before you take another step...

I'd like to drop some serious stats on you right now. 85% of the businesses started in 2000 didn't exist in the year 2010.

By the numbers, you have a 15% chance of success at this and more than likely you will fail.

Pretty grim...but it is the truth.

Some of the best advice I ever got was from my dad and it is so good I figured I would pass it along. "Don't worry about how much you can make; figure out how much you can afford to lose."

There is a good chance opening a brewery _won't work out_ for you. How much can you AND YOUR FAMILY afford to lose? $10,000...$300,000...$50?

This is important to figure out. If you are putting your life savings into this and you have no way of ever recouping it back, you may want to reconsider your plan or get more partners in your project.

It doesn't matter if your idea is great because breweries close EVERY YEAR. One of them could be yours. Have a plan where this DOESN'T work. If it doesn't, is your life still in order?

Prepare yourself and your business for success, but have an exit plan in place in case this doesn't work.

Buying Supplies

There are a handful of suppliers for breweries in the USA.

My advice: find one that is close to you. This saves on shipping costs and these can add up over time.

Grain is 'cheap', but you are using thousands of pounds a year and your shipping expenses will get pretty high pretty quick. If each shipment you get goes from California to Maine, you are going to pay more than if it went from Massachusetts to Maine.

In a perfect world, you can pick them up yourself (like I do) and really save on shipping.

One other bit of advice: When you are devising your recipes, check to see if the hops you want are readily available.

If you want a Nelson Sauvin, Huell Melon, Simcoe®, Mosaic® hopped IPA and you don't have contracts for the materials you need, then you can scrap that idea.

If your flagship beer has a rare hop, get contracts NOW, not later. Many of these sell out *before* they are even harvested.

For hops like cascade or something that is grown in bulk, you can probably spot order. But for the exotic stuff, you need to plan ahead.

Also, make sure you have ample space to store all of this stuff. Many people never take the time to put a storage area in the brewery design. Grain takes up space, so plan for it.

Most of the suppliers will not share their price list until you get your federal brewer's number, but a few will. You can price shop, but most suppliers charge the same for their products; your savings will be on shipping.

Outside of brewing supplies, remember that people will use toilet paper, napkins, glasses, etc. Find a supplier for restaurant supplies. There are hundreds of these and probably several local to you.

A lot of you are probably saying "Duh, I knew that." No you didn't. This is one of the number one items people overlook when starting the brewery business. They forget to price out their supplies.

They panic over the costs of the building, the rent, glasses, staff, etc. They almost never cost out their supplies. Over time this COULD be your number one variable cost...don't overlook it.

Licensing

Hooray! The locals approved your plan! You now have your location, and you have chosen your system.   Now you need the state and federal approvals.

First, here are a few quick stories about licensing before we get into the nuts and bolts of it:

I'm going to say something that will probably piss you off. This is the easiest part of the process. I know...you are thinking this guy is an idiot. EVERYONE has told you licensing is a royal pain in the ass and nearly impossible. I have read several blogs of people who are thinking of starting a brewery and they heard it's a bitch. I am here to tell you that information is simply not true.

I've done this twice…it is not hard and I hate even writing about it because it is that easy.

There are NO trick questions on the licensing forms. It is not the job of these agencies to deny your license; they WANT you to get your license.

Here are the two best bits of advice you will ever read regarding licensing. If you don't do these it could be tricky:

ONE: Print out all the forms you need. READ THEM TWICE before you fill-out any of them.

TWO: Call the licensing agency if you have a question.

I know that 90% of you will not do these two steps and email me with, "So how much is the federal license?" Right there, I know you didn't do step one because there is no cost to the federal licensing.

A "student" of mine came in for a brewery consultation and was all ready to go. He got his space and then was moving to licensing. He gave me a call and said he was stuck on licensing. I asked if he had printed it out, the answer was, "No". I asked if he called the Liquor Control Board to see what he needed since he was too busy to go online and read, and the answer was," No". He actually wanted to pay me to do the licensing since he was so frustrated. I said I wouldn't do that, just give me five minutes on the phone...

After FIVE MINUTES of talking to him we surfed the licensing websites and he was caught up <u>and finished his state and federal apps THE NEXT DAY in less than two hours.</u>

This isn't rocket science, so please don't make it that. If you graduated from high school, this should be very easy. They ask questions, and you answer them.

 Now, on with the licensing!

Ok, you have your space and it's cool with the locals so now you can actually get to brewing beer.   Remember, you can't apply to have a brewery until you get the space!

You will need a federal and state license to start a brewpub. MOST states like you to have (or at least have already started the process of getting) your federal license before you apply at the state level, so let's start there.

Federal Brewing License

After you read this chapter I beg you to go to www.ttb.gov. This is the website for the Alcohol and Tobacco Tax and Trade Bureau of the United States. EVERYTHING YOU NEED for your federal license is there.

But before you start, you will need an EIN (Employment Identification Number) from the IRS. This is an SS-4 form and there is no cost to get it; you can even do it online in a few minutes. You'll need this number on about every page of your apps.

I bet you want 40 pages of details on what to do for your license...that would be overkill. Depending on what you are doing, there are five to eight separate forms to fill out. None are worth giving instructions for. Print them, read them, complete them.

One item that DOES cost money is the Brewers Bond. This is required by the TTB so that if you default on your tax payments, they will still get their money. For your size, it will LIKELY be $100 a year over four years. There are hundreds of places online that sell these bonds so they are very easy to obtain.

You'll also need a sketch of your place. You can do this yourself, but if you have an architect you can just upload the drawings with your application.

That's it; don't make it harder than you have to. It's just paper with some questions. Read them and answer them. It couldn't be easier.

True Story #4: I mentioned my friend Kasey Turner of Jailbreak Brewing earlier and here is a quick story I have from him. He was visiting my brewery and was telling me he just got his Federal license approved. He then said this, *"You were dead wrong on telling me how easy licensing was."* I was a little taken aback by this. Then he said, *"It was much easier than you led on."*

Seriously, it is that easy.

State License

The last time I checked, there were 50 states. I'm not going into detail about each state, but I will give some tips on what to look for…

Do the same thing here and print out the forms. Read them, understand them.

Find the state's liquor code. Read what it says about brewpubs. Now, I know that they are filled with legal bullshit, but they are worth reading. If there is something you truly don't understand and think it may affect your application, please call the state and ask.

Next are health inspections. Some states put beer brewing under their agriculture department and they actually inspect your brewery similar to that of a restaurant.

Some states (and local communities) are very concerned about what you are doing with water, so more work may be required here. This is usually done at the local level, but be prepared for some additional paperwork.

Also, check on the cost of your license. Some states charge $500 a year while others charge $4,000 a year. This could drastically affect your start up costs, so it's worth finding out NOW...not later.

Also, if one of your choices was to have other beer, wine, and/or spirits, start looking into what licenses you need for those and what the costs of those are.

Again...PRINT OUT THE FORMS AND READ THEM! This will make filling them out so much easier.

Brewer's Note: I know you're thinking these last few pages were a waste of time. This was all common sense. Well, I've said it before, and I'll say it again...common sense is not all that common.

If common sense were so damn common, no one would ever "accidently" get pregnant; order oysters at a truck stop in Denver; sleep with the secretary; or watch an Adam Sandler movie.

But common sense isn't all that common...

- *Homework #6* - **Take this advice: print out the forms, do the homework, and research. You will be 10 miles ahead of your competitors.**

Creating a Buzz

Ok, you got your license, your space, and you are doing the construction right now. Sure, people will be walking past your place and will know when you are open, but what about everyone else?

Don't start getting the word out about your place five days before you open. Start spreading the word about two months before you open.

I know you already created all your social networking sites. You should also "build" your presence on those sites. As you are "building" your pub, put pictures online. Give updates on the progress.   Talk about the beers you are going to have opening night. Introduce your brewer.

All of this should tell the story of your "rise in the community". People like seeing others invest in their backyard. Show your investment VISUALLY.

I also want you to call the local newspaper. Your business is pretty cool and probably the only one in town, so your local paper would love to hear about it.

Also reach out to the regional beer bloggers. They have an audience and can help get the word out to their following.

We will get more into marketing in a few pages, but this is a timeline...after you get approvals start getting customers!

Hiring Staff

You may or may not have ever paid someone to do work for you before. And, no, paying the neighbor kid 10 bucks to cut your lawn doesn't count as you being an employer.

This can be pretty scary. You have to interview people, hire them, pay them, etc. We will get into managing them in a bit, but first you need to find them. From start to finish, I will tell you some things that do work and some that don't work.

How much staff do you need?

This is a tough one to figure out, but you need to write it down. If there is food, you are going to need a cook, dishwasher/busboy, wait staff, hostess, and maybe a manager.

If you know nothing about food, you better bring in a chef who has run a kitchen before. Chefs don't come cheap or often, but will be worth it to you.

If you aren't brewing the beer, you're going to need a head brewer and maybe a few assistant brewers on staff.

If you went the route of full service bar, you'll have to have a trained mixologist on staff.

Write down your staff needs and this will help you with the next step...

My advice is to go a little heavy with your service staff (bartenders, waitresses, hostess, etc) to start. Wages are cheap and a few will probably quit early on anyway.

The reason you go heavy is because you have no idea how busy you will be to start. Regardless of how packed your place is, people will leave pissed off if they aren't taken care of properly. If you have one bartender taking care of 85 people, they will be waiting...and waiting.

Some may wait so long they go off to another bar and never come back to yours.

Advertise Your Openings

It isn't 1930. Putting a "Help Wanted" sign on your building will not bring hundreds of qualified applicants.

For specialized hires (chefs, trained bartenders), try the local training centers for these professions. Many have lifetime job placement and will help you find applicants.

If you need a brewer or brewer's assistant, there are several brewing magazines and online sites that have postings on this. Also contact your state brewer's guild. They may know of a brewer who was just let go or one who wants to leave.

Post your jobs on the internet somewhere other than craigslist.com. I have nothing against craigslist; I think it is a great site. I even hired someone from a post I put there. But I can tell you that you will probably be able to pick out most of your "craigslist people" about 10 seconds into questioning.

There are hundreds of places to post jobs but don't forget some other hidden places that yield some nice results: unemployment offices, community centers, church bulletin boards, etc.

Most importantly, ask your friends and family. They aren't going to refer someone to you they think will suck.

Paying them

Yes, they probably will want paid for their services. The Brewers Association® has some great payroll surveys that it makes available to members. It details what the average salaries are from head brewers to wait staff. I highly recommend becoming a member so you have access to these materials.

The Interview

Ask honest questions and get honest answers. Be yourself and the interviewees will be themselves. That's a great place to start.

And don't ask easy questions. Too many, "What are you good at?" questions won't tell you too much. You need a few, but the best way to gauge future behavior is to ask questions about SPECIFIC PREVIOUS BEHAVIOR. "Tell me about a specific moment in a previous job when you did not get along with a co-worker. How did you handle that?"

If they go on for 30 minutes about some drama-filled incident that involved their whole office then this may not be a good fit.

Here are a few more questions I always like to ask and why:

"What is the worst decision you have ever seen a manager make? What did you do to make the best of it?"

This shows whether they pay attention to details and can work with difficult employees.

"What do you want to get out of this place?"

Do you have a go-getter who wants to run his own brewery? A waitress who wants to work her way through school and get a better job?   You never know. A red flag for me is the answer "cash". If that's all someone wants, then there are a lot of opportunities to "take" a little extra cash here.

"I want you to find all of the gas stations in the city of Chicago and provide me with a list of them by the end of the week. How would you do this?"®

That's right, I am copywriting this one because I like it so much. So why ask this? It requires critical thinking in a situation where people are not prepared with answers.

This person thought he was getting beer and food questions, and you just asked about gas stations in Chicago.   Best answers go along the lines of..."Well, I'd go to Google® and type in "Chicago Gas Stations" and print you out a report in about five minutes."

This shows he had a week, but got it done now.

Bad answer would be, "I would go to Chicago, drive up and down each street in the city and start a chart with all of the gas stations listed." So you're going to use MY MONEY to go to Chicago and spend a few days out there to get all of this info? That's a waste of time and money.

"What did you do last weekend?"

If the answer was smoke weed and egg houses, you may want to cut the interview short. This is a great way to determine behavior, and get personal life info without asking personal questions.

"What is the worst day you have ever had at work?"

Was it his fault? Was it because her "boss was an idiot"? This is always a red flag question for me. If it was the "boss was an idiot" path, then guess what, she will probably think you're an idiot too.

"You look overqualified. Why do you want to work here?"

They may tell you they aren't all that qualified. (Yes, that has happened.). They may also tell you they love craft beer and would do anything to work in the industry. They may tell you that they were fired from all five of the jobs on their resume so their qualifications aren't all that good.

"Which one of your references (or previous employers) can't I call?"

Be direct. You are telling them you assume they are going to say not to call a few even when they know they shouldn't.

If it is a current employer, you need to respect that. If they say, "please don't call xxx," ask why. You may learn something here. A good answer would be that you can call any of them.

Some other quick tips: Make them answer your question. This isn't a presidential debate where you can blabber for 90 seconds and not answer the question because of time. If they say, "I don't know of anything off the top of my head," tell them you'll give them a few minutes.

Ask for previous specific examples. Make them say specifically what they did in a tough situation, not what they would do, but what they actually did. If you have worked for 12 consecutive months at one place, you have dealt with a tough situation.

True Story #5: "Sandwich-Gate"

This is probably my favorite interview story.   It has nothing to do with beer but just shows that if you ask the right questions, you can learn all you ever wanted from someone.

One question I generally ask is, "When was the last time you were fired? What happened?"

My favorite answer was what I now refer to as "Sandwich-Gate". Here is a word for word breakdown of this young man's answer...

"Well, I took a late lunch around 12:15 one day. I go to heat up my cup-o-soup and BOOM! There is a sandwich just sitting in the microwave. I touched it and it was cold.

I thought – this must be from yesterday – I took it out and heated up my soup.

*I came back around 12:45 and guess what? The sandwich is **still there**! I keep thinking – there is NO way this is from today – I was pretty damn hungry and...I mean who is taking a lunch after 12:45? Anyways, I heat up the sandwich and start eating it. Now it's AT LEAST 12:50 right now, and guess what?*

The bitch that owns that sandwich walks in and sees me eating it. She flips out, starts screaming. I offered to cut off the area that I had bitten int,o but that wasn't good enough for "Princess".

*Long story short, I was terminated for 'breaking company policy', whatever the f*ck that means."*

Seriously, this happened to me when I was looking to fill a position at the brewery. While it doesn't provide too much info on opening your brewery, it does teach one lesson. Let people talk; you never know what they are going to say.

Marketing, PR, Websites, and Getting People in the Door

Everyone has seen *Field of Dreams* with Kevin Costner...

"If you build it...they will come."

Unfortunately, that is NOT the case with brewpubs. People won't magically know that Ty Cobb, Babe Ruth, and your dead Dad are drinking at your bar unless you tell them.

So what is the best way to do that? I can't stress enough that there isn't ONE way to do this. You have to diversify.

Believe it or not, not everyone uses the internet to search for breweries. Nor does everyone read the local brewing newsletter. But some people do a little of each.

I have it laid out pretty extensively on what you SHOULD do. Please, if you have better ideas use them.

Here's a little quote I USE ALL OF THE TIME and it angers people every time they hear it. Good Tasting beer doesn't matter.

Don't believe me?

Check a few beer rating websites. Look at the bottom 15 to 30 beers on the site. I can almost guarantee that most beers on that list are some of the best selling beers in the United States.

So why does someone who makes GREAT beer have a market share of less than .01%, and some huge brewery that makes turd-tasting beer own over 33% of the beer market?

In three words: Advertising, Marketing, and PR.

It's true. You can make beer that doesn't taste good to beer drinkers and you can sell more of that than great tasting beer because you position it correctly.

Getting back to the point of this story...You need to advertise and get your story out there.

Most people don't have too much experience here. I've done marketing for non-profits, constructing companies, newspapers, and my brewery. I also went to school for four years for this...I have an idea how to do it, so take it for what it is worth.

With that said, I will tell you that it doesn't matter if you don't have a business degree because EVERYONE who buys something is a marketing expert.

You picked your car for the great MPG; you picked your frozen TV dinner because of NEW CRANBERRY SAUCE! You picked your Computer because it was so damn cool...something SOLD you on these purchases.

You need to do the same with your beer. SELL IT.

Social Media Websites

Yep, people actually use these sites. Some use them quite a bit. I am going to focus on three and break them down for you.

Facebook® - To some people this is their lifeline. They conduct searches here, chat with people, and make their weekend plans on the website. There are even some new apps that make it even better for business.

Setting up a Facebook® account is very easy, so easy I won't detail it. There are some tips to get more "Likes" though.

But what should you post here? Most important thing my "followers" enjoy about my page is that I am always updating the tap list. Whenever a new beer goes on, I post it.

I even post when I am brewing a special beer so people know it is coming.

I have noticed many breweries add info about events/bands that are coming up and I use it for that, also.

You will find that many people make their weekend plans ON YOUR PAGE. They will send your posts to friends and say, "Wanna go there tonight?"

Give them a reason to go there. That is what Facebook®
should be used for if you want to maximize your
effectiveness with it.

Twitter® - No one really uses Twitter...do they?

The answer is yes. Yes, they do. And quite a few do. It
varies, but the average counts you will find list 200 million
people as "regular" users of Twitter®.

There is no cost to join, so why the hell haven't you?

It takes a bit of getting used to, and honestly, I get way
more business from Facebook as opposed to Twitter, but
the price is right so I use both.

Now, even if you suspect you won't have an "active"
Twitter account, you need to create one anyway. There
are many beer apps out there that link up to your Twitter
account.

At the very least, you can list your name and address on
your profile. That way people can search for it.

I may not sound enthused about the site, but it is a good
tool. While I don't get much business from Twitter, I do
get some. I spend about five minutes a week on the site
and probably get one person a week into my place
because of my "tweets".   Well worth five minutes of
work...

More people are using it daily as a search tool as opposed to Google or Yahoo search engines. Don't miss out on it or you will miss out on customers.

The Other Sites – There are other social media sites?

There are only about a million more.   But they really don't hold a candle to the first two.   Google+™ is picking up steam, but still doesn't have the following of Facebook.

MySpace® is working to get back all of the market share it lost and adding new features for businesses.

There are even more. And while you can't do everything, I would at least look into creating a few home pages on these other sites. It doesn't hurt.

Social Media Wrap-up: Here are my thoughts on social media. I think it is an INVALUABLE tool in getting people into my brewpub. I'd say at least 1 out of 9 people come into the bar because they saw us on one of the sites. (Yes, I do keep track; more on that later.) That would be an 11% drop in business if I didn't use them. I can't afford that and neither can you.

I am very much of the "less is more" approach on social media. Some brewers post a tweet every ten damn minutes. To me that is worthless. If you tweet 50-plus times a day, who is reading each one? Your mom may be the only one.

Keep your posts/tweets relevant to YOUR BEER. I repeat... **Keep your posts/tweets relevant to YOUR BEER**!

The one tweet you want people to read, "Barley Wine getting tapped this weekend!", will get lost in the shuffle of your, "Cats Rule and Dogs Drool! #catsareawesome" tweets you are always posting.

If people want to know about Obamacare, they aren't running to see what your opinion is on the topic. If you post your views on the topic all you are going to do is alienate people. People want to KNOW ABOUT YOUR BEER!

If you waste their time with non-beer info, I can assure you that you won't get too much business from your social media.

Also, try to post different info on each site. Many people use both and if you cut and paste a tweet to your Facebook feed it will annoy them because they got it twice.

Homework #7: **Go to five brewpubs' Twitter® and Facebook® pages. Then go to mine...what "worked" for you? Which one would you most likely visit if they were all a ten minute drive from your house and why? How**

many times a week do I post? How many times a week do others post?

Website

Beyond social media, you *NEED* your own website. I know several brewpubs that don't have one. They use their social media pages as their website.   That's a mistake.

You may think that could work for you, but let me tell you why you need a site.

My dad would NEVER go to Twitter.com or Facebook.com…NEVER.   I can't even imagine a scenario where he would *accidently* go to either site.

He does, however, use the internet all of the time, and he does drink beer.

Beyond that, search engines prefer you having your own site more than just a Facebook page. When people type in your brewery's name, there is a much better chance your own website will pop up #1 in rankings than some irrelevant web address.

Starting and maintaining a website can cost as little as $120 a year. Check out www.beaverbrewingcompany.com. I do the site all by myself and it took me about two days to get it set up. I spend another ten minutes a week keeping it updated.

Some brewpubs pay thousands of dollars to get a "good" website. You can do that, but this is one avenue I say to go cheap. You aren't selling an online product so you don't need a ton a pictures and flash® to entice people to pay right then and there. You just need them to get in your door.

A bit of advice on web pages: You have a very cool business and there are A LOT of people out there who are in the web page design business. Many are very fresh and eager to grow their portfolios.

I have (and this is no exaggeration) been offered a completely new web design by a professional at LEAST 15 times. I turn it down each time because I actually like how mine runs and am happy with the results. But if you want to go the pro route, you may be able to get one for free.

Homework #8: **Check out 3-4 brewpub websites including mine @ www.beaverbrewingcompany.com and see what works for you.**

Marketing

Even though you are selling your beer in-house, you will need a theme. Is your beer badass? Are you going to have nothing but dark beers? Are you doing all sour beers? Are you doing all of the above?

If you have a business degree you will undoubtedly have heard what I am writing next:

You're not the first person to make a beer. You are what we call a "late adopter". What does someone who has joined an industry late in the game have to do to stay in business and compete?

Be Better, Be Cheaper, or Be Different. Hopefully, all three.

Marketing covers the "Be Different" part. You need to start positioning your brewpub as "different" from the others. If you do everything the same as everyone else, guess what? There is no incentive to go to *your* place.

Here is an example of being different...Just about all pubs have sample platters. They are generally on a long wooden board or "ski".

Instead of opting to do whatever everyone else is doing (and saving a ton of money in the process), I made my own. I bought a branding iron with my logo, and cut the wood in the shape of Beaver County, the county where my pub is located and also the name of the brewery.

Locals love this and often ask if they can buy them. They look cool, serve a purpose, and no one has ever seen one like this before.

This is what I am talking about: do something unique. It doesn't have to be crazy but it needs to be YOURS.

This isn't homework, but I want you to sit there for a moment and think of the "vibe" of your place and your beer. What theme are you going for?

Are you going for the barn rustic feel? The big city uptown feel? The taproom inside a huge brewery feel? Whatever it is, you need to align the rest of your thinking around that idea so you have a consistent message.

I myself have a very non-pretentious place and theme. There aren't 300 posters up in my bar. There aren't the coolest, trendiest bands there (I have no live entertainment, ever); there isn't expensive furniture to sit down and read poetry.

What I do have is a laid back atmosphere. There are pictures of all the staff behind the wall of the bar. People don't yell, "Hey, you!" They refer to people by their names.

Either I or the bartender shakes the hand of each person who comes in and introduces him/herself and says thanks for stopping in. We all make an effort to remember the name of everyone who comes in the place as well. (Yes, this is marketing...it's called "branding".)

We never tell people what beer they will like or dislike. They have their own taste buds and they can decide. We do, however, tell them what *we* like to drink. I beg people not to try our sour beers.

I truly hate anything sour in beers and I tell people that. It hasn't deterred one person from buying them when they are on tap, though. People appreciate the honesty.

We have pinball machines instead of pool tables.

Our sound system pumps out 90's and 00's hip-hop, (*A Tribe Called Quest, Warren G, Nice and Smooth* etc.), 80's hits (Madonna, George Michael, Michael Jackson), and one-hit wonders.

We don't have a cash register. All the change is made from the pockets of whoever is working.

All of these little things go into the marketing theme of having a laid back place that is fun to hang out at with friends.

Think about the experience you want people to have when they come in. Now take that idea and take it across your website, social media, bar, and everything else attached to your brewery.

If you aren't the artsy type, it may help to get an artist/graphic designer to help you with a logo or color scheme for your place. A professional can also design a sign for the outside of your place.

Mine is as simple as can be...

That's it; no frills, just a black and white sign on a white building. (Which has had some updates since the pic, but you get the idea.)

You may want lights, bells, whistles, and the whole nine yards.

Whatever you choose, make sure it goes with your theme.

Which brings up an important marketing tip...make sure everything meshes together. If you have a black and white logo, make your webpage black and white...and your shirts...maybe even the paint on your walls. Have everything flow together.

If your webpage is red and black, your logo is blue and yellow, and your sign is orange and white, people won't associate one with the other. Have everything look the same (even the same font), and people will associate anything with that font/colors as yours.

Wise words of wisdom on the internet and marketing...

"If you want to listen to an asshole speak, just fart."
-    Dan Woodske

Yes, I just wrote that. And quite honestly, I think it is great advice. I am going to tell you something that may hurt your feelings, but it shouldn't...

People are going to think you, your beer, and your place suck. And they are going to feel empowered to go online and tell a whole bunch of strangers how bad you suck.

My advice...get over it. As long as you see repeat customers, have people tell you they enjoyed their visit, and get good feedback about your beer...you are doing just fine.

Inevitably, there will be the person who comes in and is just a hater. He didn't like your jeans and thought a Kolsch with Czech Saaz Hops and not German Saaz Hops is just stupid.

Just wanted to let you know that there WILL BE negative feedback somewhere about your place. Not because your place sucks, but because there are assholes out there who hate everything.

Also, what you should try to do is fix whatever issue a person may have BEFORE he leaves. Is he making a weird face after trying a beer or food? Ask him if it is okay. If it isn't, fix the problem.

Constantly ask people if they are enjoying their time. Ask how you can improve it. If you see 10 people put on their jackets while they are there, ask them if you should turn up the heat.

I'm not saying disregard all feedback. If you constantly get negative feedback, you have a problem. If once a month someone *anonymously* writes something on the internet, you don't have a problem.

What I do want to say is, don't let it get to you. Don't obsess over it. A lot fewer people actually read those postings than you think might.

Do you think Bill Gates sits up at night and reads blogs with people ripping Microsoft®?

Seriously, envision Bill Gates scouring message boards wondering why *Buxton6969* thinks that the Xbox isn't cool. It doesn't bother him and shouldn't bother you. Just want to let you know that it will exist so you're prepared for it.

Public Relations

Yes, this is different from marketing, and you should start working on this BEFORE you open and continue thereafter.

Now, I have a background in business so I sometimes talk about this stuff like you already know what it is so let's take this slow.

What exactly is "Public Relations"? A dictionary definition is something like this... *"The professional maintenance of a favorable public image by an organization or a famous person."*

The key phrase is "maintenance of a favorable public image". The easiest way to explain this is to look at politics. You don't buy anything from politicians, however, they advertise on TV and the radio ALL THE TIME. Politicians may have pictures taken of themselves cleaning the side of the road, volunteering at an old people's home, helping kids search for Easter eggs...something to improve their public image.

You need to do this, too. It can be done in a million different ways, but let's look at some more popular ones.

1. Local Press

A great place to start is your local newspaper. Let them know your plans BEFORE you open. A good time to contact them would be while construction is going on. Let them know you are hiring people, spending money to improve the neighborhood, and going to do your part to improve the community by doing (insert your idea here.)

Also check out local magazines, beer bloggers, and other traditional media outlets. They are already known in the community, and getting an endorsement from them could be a big push for you.

2. Donate your time

Is there a local fundraiser going on in your community? If there is, this is a great time to get all decked out in gear from your brewery and donate your time to help out with whatever needs done. Again, this puts a positive image of you and your company out there. A popular thing to do now is to "Adopt a Highway" and clean it up two or three times a year.

3. Target your audience

While the newspaper is great, you will probably reach a whole bunch of non-beer drinkers. There is no better way to get fans of your place than having them try your beer. Many breweries that aren't yet licensed show up at brewfests and serve their beer. This is a great way to get more than just the word out about your place.

4. Introduce yourself to the Police and Fire Department.

God forbid they ever have to come to your place but they may have too. And if they do you want them to be familiar with your place.

It's also a courtesy for them...they don't want to be coming into your building during a fire not knowing where anything is located.

It also doesn't hurt that you are bringing in 5-10 people that live/work in your community into your place before it opens. I am sure they will like it...I know the people in Beaver Falls appreciated it.

My PR Story:

I make Kvass at the brewery. It is an ancient Russian beverage made from Bread, Lemons, and Raisins.

I made a batch a few years ago and a buddy of mine said I had to submit this to *BeerAdvocate™ Magazine*. I really didn't want to do this.

Kvass is a really unique beverage and at 1.4% ABV, it isn't really something that *BeerAdvocate* people are really into, but I said if he paid for the shipping I would send them a sample. We did and I am glad I did.

It was the first (and to my knowledge) only Kvass they have ever reviewed in the magazine. They called it "an amazing beer," which I was very pleased to read.

Surprisingly enough, there were about a dozen people I had never seen before in the brewery that weekend after the review just because they saw it in the magazine. They never knew I was in existence so close to them but read that article and had to make the trip.

You can have a story similar to this. If you think your beer is up to task, send it to a few beer review magazines/sites. If you get some good press, it could be some very good PR for your company. Just know that someone could also blast it for being terrible. There is a risk/reward but this is something you should at least consider. It helped me out and I am glad I did it...Even though I was sweating it out for a few months until I saw it in print!

The "One and Done" Beer drinker

Not sure this is an actual term but if not I just invented it. I have found that there are many "One and Done" beer drinkers. These are the drinkers who want to have one of whatever you make just so they can say they have had it, or to write a review online at ratebeer.com or beeradvocate.com.

While this is a small percentage of the beer drinking market, it does exist. I have a few dozen people who pop into my brewery once every month or so and only try the new beers.

I ask what they like and they tell me, "The Brown Note is one of my favorite beers of all-time!" I ask if they want a glass and they kindly decline just so they can try my new XXX beer.

Understand that there are these drinkers out there. Give them a reason to keep coming in by updating your beer list online at all times. They may only come in if something is new.

Also, let them know about the specifics on your beer like ABV, IBU's, etc. If they are posting to beer review websites, they will want this info.

Why you really shouldn't skip the previous sections on selling your beer...

Seriously? You flipped ahead because you thought this stuff didn't matter? If it didn't matter, the 50 best selling beers in the United States wouldn't exist. Do yourself a favor...take a look at the top 50 selling beers...do you drink any of them? I doubt it. But they sell a whole hell of a lot more than you'll ever sell in a year and they do it through marketing, advertising, and PR. Don't take it lightly...IT MATTERS!

Running Your Brewpub

You may remember all the way in the beginning of the book that I mentioned that I have an area of study in organizational behavior. This was very helpful when I became CEO of Beaver Brewing Company.

There will be other people at the brewery other than you and if they are working there they will be taking direction from you. If you don't give them direction, they won't do anything.

Think of where you work. What happens when the boss isn't there? Who takes charge? Do people work harder? Do they slack off? Is your boss a task master? Or laid back?

How are you going to run the place?

There are several ways to run your place which I will go over, but let me tell you how I run my place.

First off, I find good people who fit with my personality. I want people who want to run the place themselves and need little direction. I want people who can make decisions instantly when it comes to customer service.

I have an interview question I always ask: *"Someone comes in, orders a beer. He tells you this is the worst thing he has ever tasted. What do you say to him?"*

The answer I normally get... *"Why didn't you like it?"*

I hate that answer. I want this one. *"Let's get you a new one then, and I won't charge you for either one. So, what type of beer do you normally drink? Have you ever tried our sampler?"*

I don't care why they didn't like it. They didn't like it; that's all that matters. Don't question someone's own taste buds. Customers will resent that.

I don't want to lose a customer over a $4 beer. People always remember GREAT or CRAPPY experiences at places where they eat and drink. Give them great service. I also want to get them to find something they do like on tap so I always suggest our sample platter. I haven't had a customer go through that and NOT enjoy at least three of the five beers.

I tell the people who work for me to pretend they own the place and don't let a customer leave with a bad experience.

If someone spills beer at the bar, the first thing we do is....before I get to that what would you do?

Would you clean up the spill? Hand them paper towels?

I would do one of those, but only after I handed them another full beer. Don't charge them for two...it probably costs you around $1 for that beer, but you'll earn about $30 in goodwill from that customer. And your bartender will appreciate the tip left, also.

I only want people to work at the bar who are 100% committed to the customers. If they aren't, they don't work there...or at least not for long.

That brings me to another point...know when to let go.

If the employee sucks don't keep him/her on your staff. How many places have you worked where most of the people you worked with sucked at their job? I worked at several.

The boss/owners knew these people sucked but kept them around because they didn't like to fire people. The company suffered and your spouse had to listen to you gripe about that shitty employee every night at the dinner table. No one wins when a bad employee stays on staff.

Here's a newsflash: No one LIKES to fire people, but to be successful you have to.

You have a place where people are dying to work at (believe me, people really want to work in the brewery business and will even take less cash to do so), so if you have bad employees there are 20 people behind them who can do and want to do their job.

Side Note: You have figured out by now whether you like the style that this book is written (I sure hope so). I am writing to you just like I talk to people on the other side of the bar...like normal human beings. If you stop in the pub to grab a beer and shoot the shit you will get the same guy that wrote this book and vice versa.

I take customer service the same way. Treat people like humans and exactly how you would want treated.

Side Note #2: I hate kids...not in general...but I do hate them in a bar. My place is for adults. I serve beer and wine. There is no room for kids in there. All they will do is take away from the vibe I have going in there. Sorry if that bums you out, but I don't want some seven year-old wining that the place is boring and why Sponge Bob wasn't on TV. I can' t tell you how many patrons thank me for not allowing kids in the place. Just some food for thought....

True Story #6: Had an employee one time who was CONSTANTLY breaking my #1 rule: Introduce yourself to each bar patron and if possible, shake his hand.

After **several reminders** this employee just wouldn't do it. I literally reminded him as customers walked in and he "forgot". Halfway into this person's second day, I asked this person to go home. Told him he wasn't cut out for this and thanks for his time.

Usually, I can tell in one day if it will work out or not. I gave this person two, and this person wasn't working.

Moral of the story: If people aren't working for you, they shouldn't be working for you.

Here's another question for you...how often will you be there?

I am physically at the brewery at least six days a week. Since I am the brewer, manager, marketing department, janitor, etc, I do everything there. I also help out bartending each night.

People at the bar really enjoy having the brewer/owner (me) there when they are. They can ask questions about the place, the beer. And quite honestly, I enjoy talking to them.

I can find out immediately what beers are selling well, what people want to have in the future, and what they think of the place.

Do you want to be doing that? Do you like working evenings? Do you plan on ever being there? These are all questions you need to ask. Some people just want to own a place, and some want to actually work there.

Whether you believe it or not, your workers will watch you while you are there.   They also mirror what you do. If you are good with customers, they will be too.   If you suck with them, so will they.

My advice is to be there as much as possible and set an example. Business organizations take the form of their leadership...you are the leader.   Whatever type of worker you are, that's what your employees are going to be.

This *seems* like common sense, but have you ever worked at a place where your boss was an idiot? If the answer is no, then you are pretty damn lucky.

Along with making beer and selling beer, there are a lot of daily items that need to be taken care of at a brewpub.

Inventory, trips to the bank, paying employees, ordering supplies, keeping track of your tax liability, and a litany of other things.

Who will do all of this? You, or will you hire someone to do this?

After you are up and running, you are going to have to decide what type of place you want to run: A fun place, an all-business type of place, one where you are always there or never there?

Taxes

Believe it or not, you will have to pay taxes. Not just personal income taxes, but other ones as well.

Let's stick to the beer ones for now…

Federal Excise Taxes – At the size you are at, you will need to pay $7 for each BBL of beer you make. These are due quarterly. There is an easy-to-fill-out form on the TTB website.

YOU NEED TO KEEP TRACK OF WHAT YOU MAKE! Taxes need to be paid and need to be accurate. You also have to file these on time. Check out the forms on the TTB website.

State Excise Taxes – Each state differs on the amount and when you need to pay. Some are quarterly, some monthly. Either way, you have to file these just as accurately as federal ones.

State Sales Tax – Just like the excise taxes, state sales tax differs from state to state. Most states require you to have a sales tax license BEFORE you apply for your brewery license.

Payroll Taxes – There are many software companies that make some great apps that you can use to keep track of payroll and your payroll taxes. I personally use an accountant and I would recommend you use either an accountant or a payroll service to do your payroll. They are pretty cheap, and take that responsibility off your plate.

In the end, failing to pay your taxes is the easiest way to lose your license. If you don't pay your taxes, you will lose your license.

Important note - I would factor in taxes to your cost analysis. Especially property taxes (if you own). In Pennsylvania, I pay $9.48 per each sixtel I make and sale in just excise tax. You know this is coming, so make sure your projections show the tax liability.

Creating the Beer Menu

This is one of those sections you can read for some "food for thought". You may have a different plan than I do, and that's fine...many other brewpubs do it differently. I'm just sharing what I do and what my customers seem to enjoy.

First off, very few of my beers are over 5.5% ABV. This may come off as wimpy, but how am I serving all of my beer? It's all on draft and served for onsite consumption. (Minus growlers which are taken offsite.)

I don't like having too many (if any) "imperial" high ABV beers. If I did, most people would drink one, then not be able to have another because they are driving. I prefer them to have 3 – 4 beers on a visit, not just one.

This is how I set up my beer menu...

One. I don't have a flagship beer, but I do have three that are on tap year round:

I.Porter.A – Porter malts are mixed with typical IPA hop varieties for either a black IPA or a Hoppy Porter, depending on how you look at it.

Basil – An Amber Ale made with one pound of fresh basil. I'll give you one guess on what it tastes like...

Chamomile Wheat – A 4.4% ABV Wheat Hefeweizen where 16% of the "beer" is actually steeped chamomile flowers. Light, crisp, fruity, and refreshing.

I keep these on tap all the time because they are distinctively different tasting beers and they bring out the uniqueness of the brewery. My thinking is that if you like the Basil, you can't go down the road and get another basil-based beer from a large brewery...it doesn't exist anywhere else. If you like it, you have to come to my place to get it.

Two. Variety is the spice of life.

All the other beers I have rotate all of the time. Many beers I make only once a year.   My French Styled Biere De Garde is always a hit, but you won't see it on tap anytime other than the last half of June.

My Brown Note is also a crowd pleaser, but I only make it about four times a year.

One beer that is a semi-regular is my Nelson Sauvin Pale Ale. Probably about 9 out of the 12 months a year, it is available.   It's the best selling beer I have, but I do like to be "out" of it sometimes. It makes it more special.

Even if people "LOVE" a particular beer and demand it to come back, they will probably "LOVE" one of the next beers you make, too. This variety will have them coming back to find the next one they love.

Three. Saison/Kolsch combo.

Craft beer is exploding across the country, but still 90% of the beer consumed here is NOT craft beer.   These are your "bad" pilsner drinkers. And believe it or not, they will come to your place. I get them all the time. You need something for them to drink.

You don't want to hand them your Double IPA even though you think it is your best beer. They are going to hate it. You need to ease them into intensely hopped beers.

I compare it to giving 12 year-olds a black coffee. They will hate it. Give them some sugar and cream and they'll probably enjoy it.

My answer for these non-craft beer drinkers comes in two forms….the Kolsch and the Saison. April thru September I always have some sort of Saison on tap. October thru March you will see a Kolsch on tap.

These are styles of beer that I like to qualify as having nothing offensive in them. Neither are heavily hopped nor do they have a high ABV. They are the two easiest drinking styles in the craft beer world and very easy beers to serve to convert non-craft drinkers.

They also appeal to the serious craft drinker because you don't see much of either style frequently at the bottle shop. It's a treat for them, too.

If you aren't familiar with either style, give them a try; you'll be surprised how well they sell in your brewpub!

Four, Make beer for a certain audience.

On occasion, I will make a beer I know a very narrow segment of the beer drinking community will enjoy. I hate the taste of sour/wild ales, but I have one on tap from time to time.

Not many people enjoy these beers, but the ones who do really appreciate having them on tap. Few breweries and even less bars carry a serious selection of sour beers, so this is a treat for a few people.

I'd put Smoked Beers along with Chile beers into this category. Have them every once in a while and you'll be surprised to see some new people in your brewery when you have them.

Insurance

There are two groups of people in the insurance world...people who want it no matter what the price...and people who don't want it if it costs more than $5.

There are MANY types of insurance out there. Here is a brief overview of the most common ones for brewpubs:

Finished Products Liability: This covers you if you have something like the Ebola virus in your beer by accident. If someone has your product and gets sick and dies, you are covered.

General Liability: Slips, falls, accidents that happen at the brewery to people who aren't your workers. It's always a good idea to have at least $1,000,000 in coverage here.

Workers Compensation: One of your employees gets hurt at work and cannot return to work due to an injury. This insures the employee while out of work. You are required to have this...if you don't have it and someone does get hurt (or you get caught without it), you'll get fines, penalties, and be forced to buy it at a much higher price.

Property Insurance: If you own, you SHOULD have this.

Renters Insurance: This covers your equipment should there be a fire or something like that at the place you rent.

Liquor Liability: This is the most hotly debated insurance in the bar world.   This covers you in the event you over serve a patron of your bar who drives off and gets in a car accident or causes some other type of damage due to intoxication and your over -serving.

Do you get insurance or not? If you are serving hard liquor, I recommend it. If you have a bartender who loses track of who he's serving, he can over serve someone VERY quickly.

It also depends on the vibe of your place. Are you playing really loud music and encouraging people to dance? Or are you running a mom & pop type storefront and serving to locals only? Each place and business is unique...decide if you need Liquor Liability or not.

Best bet is to ask your insurance agent about your risk and if it makes sense to carry it or not.

Accounting

Have you ever run your own business? Do you have an accounting degree? Are you comfortable using accounting software? Did you go to business school?

If you have answered no to each of these questions, I would recommend getting an accountant for your business. Depending on your size, it also may not be a bad idea to consider hiring a full-time finance person to handle the day-to-day business finances.

I do most accounting myself, but I also have an accountant do a lot of things for me like payroll, year-end taxes, and other small accounting items. I also have him look at what I am bringing in and spending on a quarterly basis so I know where I am tax-wise.

Frequently Asked Questions:

These really don't fall into a category but I am asked these all the time.

Q: Do you do this full-time?

A: Yes.

Q: What's your favorite beer you don't brew?

A: Whatever is in season and, if possible, a local beer. I understand that there wouldn't be local breweries unless someone supports them. I also drink whatever is in season. I don't drink pumpkin beers in July or saisons in February. Next time you get a beer do me a favor, get one from a local brewery.

Q: What system do you brew on?

A: The custom-made Dan Woodske way. It is a 1.5 BBL system with some pumps, but pretty much it is made by me for me. Others would probably hate it.

Sure, it isn't all that efficient, but my business model is different than what most brewers use and it works for me.

Q: How much did it cost you to start your business?

A: Thanks for asking.

Q: How do you get your hops?

A: I have contracts for several of them, but I buy most of the hops whenever I need them.

Q: Where do you come up with your recipes?

A: I try to determine what is NOT being made in the beer market. Really hoppy German Oktoberfest-style beer? You never see that...so that is my late September beer. Kvass, who makes that? I do, 12 months a year. Kolsch styled beers? Not too many microbreweries pull this card, but I make it quite a bit.

Whatever doesn't exist in the market, I try to serve that market.   I read a lot about the history of beers, see how they brew beer in different corners of the world, etc. etc.

I take general beer knowledge and try to put my own twist on it. In short, I pull most of the recipes out of my ass. Throw stuff against the wall and see what sticks.

Q: How many fermenters do you have?

A: Five

Q: How much do you mark up your beer, what are your margins?

A: Wouldn't matter if I told you because the costs of my brewery are different from yours.

Closing

It took only a few hours, but you now have a pathway laid out for you to move forward with your plans of starting a brewpub.

If you get stuck on something, feel free to shoot me an email with a QUICK question to: dan@beaverbrewingcompany.com. I answer them all.

As promised, there is no "insert item A into item B and 'poof', you have a brewpub."

It is never that easy.

I did however lay the groundwork for you in an order that makes sense. Don't panic if you don't do it in this order... You may have the money before the space, the local approval before you sign the lease, the staff before your space...

I'm here to tell you that is ok. Whatever works for you works...leave it at that.

If you are ever in the neighborhood, bring in this book and I'll buy you a beer. I always love talking to perspective brewers!

Thanks

First, thanks to you for buying this book. I greatly appreciate it. You can spend your money a lot of other ways and it means a lot to me that you chose to spend yours here.

Thanks to my wife for tolerating this idea of opening a brewpub. She never liked the idea but liked me and figured that in the end I would find a way to make it work.

Thanks to my parents, my sister, and my in-laws. Without all of their help throughout the process, I wouldn't have gotten half of this accomplished.

A special thanks to my cat, Bemus. I have been unemployed three, maybe four times in my life. Each time I tried to teach myself something new. I also found that it is easy to lose your sanity while trying to teach yourself something and start a business around it. I'm not sure that bouncing brewery ideas off of my cat enhanced my sanity, but it sure didn't hurt. He was a pretty good listener and always had a good idea or two to add when the creative juices stopped flowing.

Last bit of advice...DRINK LOCAL BEER! The only way this craft beer revolution continues to grow is if you continue to fuel it. Make plans to visit brewpubs in your state.

When you meet up with friends take them to a brewery...do your part to make this work...it doesn't work without you...